MAKING WIRE JEWELRY

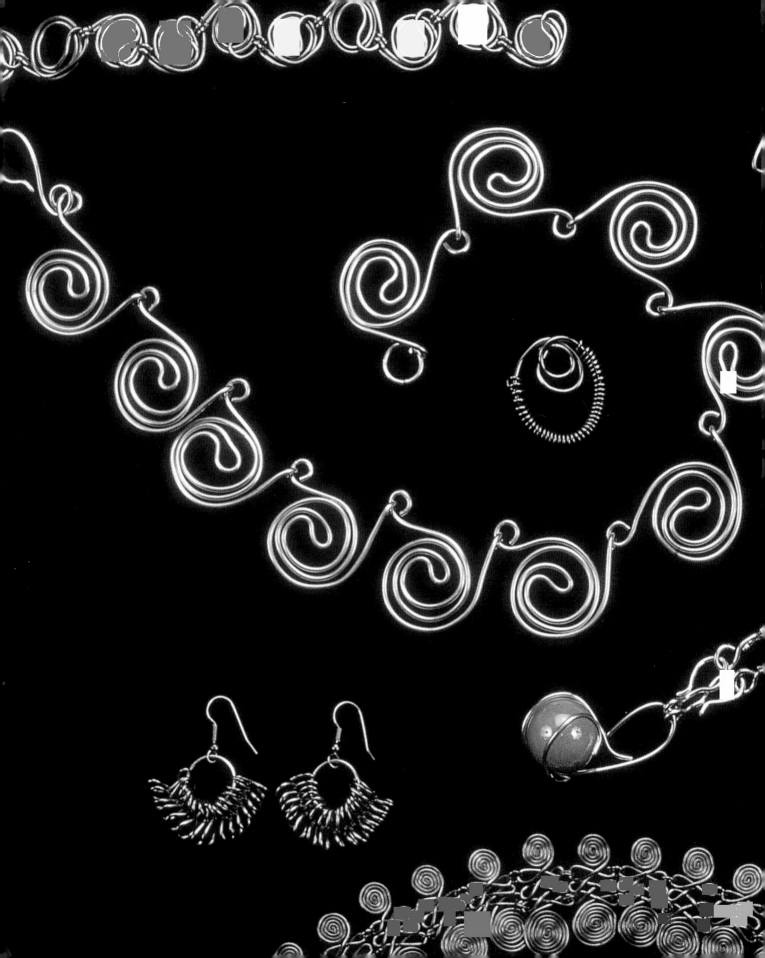

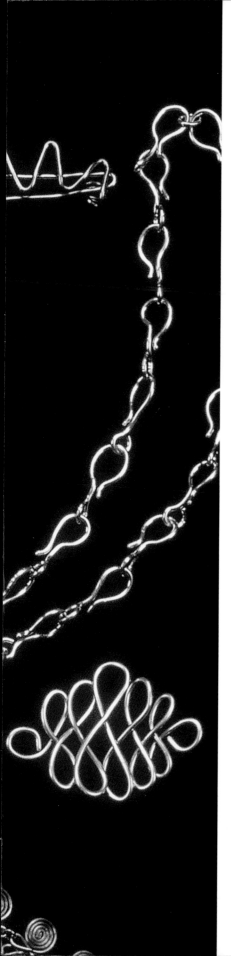

MAKING WIRE JEWELRY

MAKING WIRE JEWELRY

60 EASY PROJECTS IN SILVER, COPPER & BRASS

by Helen Clegg & Mary Larom

Lark Books
A Division of Sterling
Publishing Co., Inc.
New York

Editor: Jane LaFerla
Book Design and Production: Valentina DuBasky
Photo Styling: Dana Irwin
Photographer: Evan Bracken
Illustrations: Mary Larom

Library of Congress Cataloging-in-Publication Data Available

10 9 8 7

Published by Lark Books, a division of
Sterling Publishing Co., Inc.
387 Park Avenue South, New York, N.Y. 10016

Distributed in Canada by Sterling Publishing,
c/o Canadian Manda Group, One Atlantic Ave.,
Suite 105 Toronto, Ontario, Canada M6K 3E7

Distributed in Australia by Capricorn Link
(Australia) Pty Ltd., P.O. Box 6651, Baulkham
Hills, Business Centre NSW 2153, Australia

If you have questions or comments about this
book, please contact:
Lark Books
50 College St.
Asheville, NC 28801
(828) 253-0467

Printed in Hong Kong

1-887374-002-x

TABLE OF CONTENTS

CHAPTERS

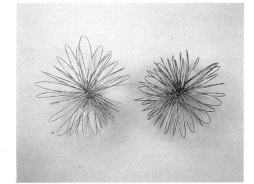

INTRODUCTION

DO YOU ADMIRE THE LOOK OF handcrafted metal jewelry? Have you flirted with the idea of creating your own but assumed the cost of tools and materials would ruin your fun? Don't wait any longer. It's time to change your outlook and get busy.

Learning to make bent wire jewelry will not only satisfy your metal hunger, you won't go broke equipping yourself or go crazy learning complicated techniques. With a few simple, readily available tools, a coil of metal wire from the hardware store, and a few hours, you can create handcrafted earrings, a bracelet, pin, or necklace with surprising ease.

BENT WIRE JEWELRY HAS BEEN A part of human adornment since man started experimenting with metal. Copper, gold, and silver were the first metals found. Brass, containing copper and zinc, was one of the first alloys. The ductile quality of these metals, their ability to be stretched or hammered into shape without breaking, allows them to be fashioned into bendable rods or threads of varying

diameters. The earliest jewelry designers quickly discovered they could use wire to create decorative pieces that were attractive, graceful, and strong.

WIRE'S APPEAL AS A JEWELRY material continues to intrigue today's artisans. Wire is flexible, easy to handle, and lends itself to almost any shape from the obviously pictorial to the completely abstract. Even the most elaborate pieces are lightweight and comfortable to wear. Wire is durable and will take a variety of finishes that enhance its look.

Wire bending does not require complicated tools or distracting machinery with hieroglyphic instructions. You can even bend it with your hands. You can teach yourself the basic techniques of wire jewelry without attending special classes or workshops. If you can identify the working end of a pair of pliers and

are adept enough to tie your shoes, you can start working.

YOU SHOULD BE AWARE OF THE one major complication of this technique—once you start creating wire jewelry, your spare time, including lunch hour and coffee breaks, may never be the same. All the components for making wire jewelry are easily portable. One woman who recently started to make wire jewelry was seen at a lecture reaching into her briefcase where she pulled out a pair of pliers, a pre-cut length of wire and began working as deftly as if she was knitting a sweater.

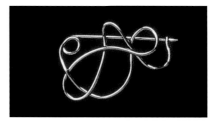

HOW TO USE THIS BOOK

YOU WILL GET THE MOST BENEFIT from this book if you complete the first nine chapters in exact order. This will enable you to master the all the techniques and skills you'll need for completing the rest of the designs in the book. Once you have learned the basics, skip through the designs, selecting the ones that appeal to you the most, or begin developing your own original ideas.

We have tested our methods of teaching with many students and have patterned this book after our classes. We know you'll have the most success if you do the designs in the order in which they appear.

Glancing at Chapter One, "An Ancient Design," you'll see that you start making a bracelet in your first lesson. While you're working on this first piece, you'll soon find that there are right and wrong ways of doing each operation—measuring, cutting, twisting, and bending wire into a well-constructed design take a bit of practice.

CHAPTER ONE IS THE LONGEST CHAPTER in the book. Don't let this scare you, work through it carefully. This chapter contains basic, introductory information that will provide step-by-step directions for first-time procedures. You will also find helpful tips about techniques, tools, and materials.

In the first few chapters we've included detailed tool and material lists to give you an indication of what you'll need for completing a

project. After that, we assume you'll know what to use and have collected what you need. We will always include the amount and gauge of wire necessary for each project as well as the size mandrel you will need if necessary.

AFTER YOU MASTER THE BASIC techniques and understand wire's limitations and possibilities, we hope you'll start thinking about designs of your own or variations of ours. Just fooling around with wire and pliers may help you to create something and, literally, you'll start adding "new twists."

Each bracelet, necklace, or belt you make will be composed of a number of links or "units." It may take several different operations to make each unit and you want them to be as alike as possible. We've found the fastest and easiest way to work is to *finish the first operation on each unit before going onto the next operation.* For instance, if you're making a bracelet of 12 links, measure and cut the wire for all 12 before starting to bend any of them. This assembly line method does two things for you:

1. You get the practice you need by learning each operation through repetition before going on to a new step.

2. You save considerable time by eliminating the extra motions required when changing tools for each new operation.

The drawings in this book are "life-size." At any step you can check your results by placing the wire you are working on against the appropriate drawing. *When you complete any operation, measure the unit against the drawing.*

There are two advantages to this method:

1. You can easily see when your work doesn't fit the pattern, allowing you to correct it before straying too far from the design.

2. Since you will measure each unit against the same drawing, they will all be alike.

ONE MORE HINT THAT WILL SAVE YOU money—until you have mastered all the fundamentals and become fairly skilled, use only copper and brass wire. Gold, silver, and anodized niobium and aluminum are so much more expensive that you will waste money if you try to learn with them.

While copper and brass are bought by the pound, silver, gold, and anodized niobium or aluminum wire are sold by the foot (centimeters) or ounce (gram). When you purchase the more costly metals, you will need to know how much you need. Therefore, we have noted the number of inches (centimeters or meters) and the correct gauge of wire for each design to help you in planning what you need.

THE BASICS: GETTING STARTED

TOOLS AND MATERIALS

The tools and materials needed for creating bent wire jewelry are very simple. Ideally, you can begin experimenting as soon as you find a length of wire and a pair of pliers. Begin your quest with a quick rummage around the family tool chest. If you have to purchase anything, a trip to the hardware store or craft supply shop should provide enough of a selection to get you started.

If you can't find what you need locally, you'll be able to obtain everything you need from a jewelry supply catalog. A few phone calls should lead you to a jewelry supply company. Request their catalog, and within a few days you'll be able to order direct.

You'll be using 18- and 20-gauge wire for your first project. All projects in this book use round wire. As you progress through the book, you'll make projects using 14-, 16-, 18- and 20-gauge wire.

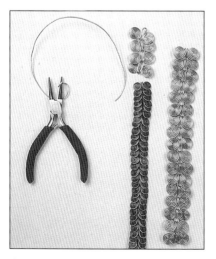

Be sure to buy wire that is soft or "annealed." Annealing is a process of heating metal then letting it cool. This softens the metal, making it easier to work. If you don't know whether the wire is annealed, try bending it. It should be relatively easy to bend without feeling stiff or brittle.

To get started, you'll need these tools and materials:

TOOLS

A pair of smooth-jawed, flat-nosed pliers *or*

A pair of smooth-jawed, parallel-action, chain-nosed pliers. (You can easily find the flat-nosed pliers at craft supply shops or hardware stores. Parallel-action pliers can be found at shops specializing in jewelry making supplies or through jewelry supply catalogs.)

A pair of smooth-jawed, round-nosed pliers

A pair of wire cutters, preferably side-cutters but diagonal cutters will also work

A small metal file (If you are buying a file ask for a small equalling file, 4-cut. If you can find them, needle files are the prefect size.)

A rubber or leather-wrapped mallet (or the smooth, broad heel of a shoe)

Knitting needles (to use as mandrels) in various sizes as specified in project directions

Jigs (You can build your own using scrap wood and nails. You will find directions for building these in the projects that use them.)

A small hand buffer (You can make this yourself by gluing some white felt on a flat stick about 12 inches (30.5 cm) long and 1 inch (2.5 cm) wide.)

Optional: mini, smooth-jawed, needle-nose pliers; small, smooth-jawed chain-nose pliers (standard, not parallel-action)

MATERIALS

1/4 pound (112 g) annealed 18-gauge round copper or brass wire

1/4 pound (112 g) annealed 20-gauge round copper or brass wire

Fine steel wool

Nonchlorine abrasive cleanser (Look for this at your grocery store. It will have calcium carbonate as its main ingredient and should not contain chlorine. Fine, powdery sand will also work.)

2 ounces (56 g) of liver of sulphur (This creates the oxidized (antique) finish. Shops selling jewelry making supplies such as a bead shop or lapidary supply shop as well as jewelry supply catalogs will carry this. You may also be able to find this through your pharmacist.)

1/2 pint (.23 l) high-grade, non yellowing, clear lacquer. (Jeweler's lacquer will give you the best results. However, you can purchase it only at shops selling jewelry making supplies or by ordering it from a jewelry supply catalog. You may also use spray lacquer but this may not give you optimum results.)

1/2 pint (.23 l) lacquer thinner

A small piece of jeweler's rouge. You can find this in shops carrying jewelry making supplies or through jewelry supply catalogs.

ABOUT TOOLS

Choosing tools is a matter of finding what you need to get the job done as well as selecting tools that are comfortable to use. The best strategy is to start with the basics and add as you go along. A pair of needle-nosed pliers for instance, which are listed as optional, may suit your touch for picking up jump rings or doing delicate work.

PLIERS

You will be amazed at the variety of pliers you'll encounter if you're shopping for new ones. Don't let this sidetrack you. For all the projects in this book you need only the smooth-jawed, flat-nosed pliers and the smooth-jawed, round-nosed pliers. Both are readily available at hardware stores or craft supply shops. If you can find them, you may want a pair of chain-nosed, parallel-action pliers (also called parallel pliers) with smooth jaws. Their advantage is a lever mechanism that keeps the jaws parallel to each other as they open and close. This gives the pliers a viselike grip that may be important to you when you are working on a coiling project or for holding the wire tight when making sharp angles. The heavier jaws of the parallel pliers may not be appropriate for more delicate work.

Smooth-jawed pliers minimize marring the surface of the metal as you work. If you already have pliers with serrated jaws, you can tape the jaws with adhesive tape to create a smooth work surface. Some jewel-

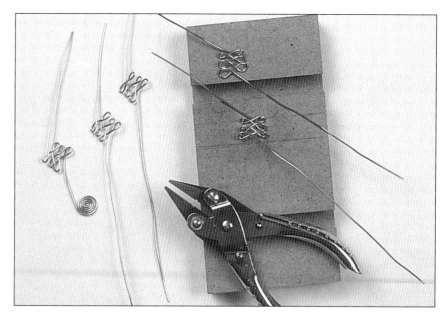

A simple homemade jig lets you twist wire to create units that are uniform in shape and size.

ers use adhesive bandages on the plier jaws, with the thicker gauze padding positioned on the inner work surface. Even when using smooth-jawed pliers you may notice some marring. Taping the jaws as described above should correct this. However, you may want to leave some marks to enhance the handmade look of a project. This is strictly a matter of personal taste for the desired finished look of the piece.

WIRE CUTTERS

Select small, side-cutters or diagonal cutters. They have sharpened blades on their interior surfaces with jaws that end in a point, allowing you to cut the wire from any side or angle. They are appropriate for delicate work.

FILES

You will need a file to smooth burrs (those rough spots left after cutting metal) or to shape the ends of wire. You will want a small, fine file. A practical shape and size for this work is an equalling, needle file, 4-cut.

MALLET

For some of the projects you will need a mallet with a rubber or leather head for hammering the individual units before assembling the piece. Unless specified, do not use a metal hammer because it will leave marks on the wire. Even if you pad the head of a metal hammer, you run the risk of marring the project. If you do not have a rubber mallet, you can use the smooth, broad heel of a shoe.

MANDRELS

A mandrel is any straight or tapered, cylindrical object around which you can bend the wire. It's used as a form for shaping wire into coils or springs. It's essential for making jump rings (small, round rings used for joining units), loops for closures, or uniform-sized units for chains.

Metal knitting needles make great mandrels. They're easy to find at any general merchandise store that has a craft section, in yarn shops, or craft supply shops. They come in a numeric sequence of sizes based on their diameter, e.g., a #3 (US) knitting needle is much thinner than a #15 (US). Projects using mandrels will specify the size knitting needle you should use.

JIGS

A jig is a form made to guide wire into a predetermined shape. By bending pre-cut lengths of wire in a repeating pattern on a jig, you can make individual units that are uniform in size and shape. You can construct your own and will find instructions for building jigs in the projects that use them.

ABOUT WIRE

Until the Middle Ages, wire was produced by hammering the metal into shape using a form. Since then, and continuing today, wire is made by the metal being "drawn" through successively smaller holes in a "drawplate" until it reaches the desired size known as a "gauge." The lower the gauge number the thicker the wire—14-gauge wire is much thicker than 24-gauge wire. All projects in this book use round wire.

We recommend that you create the projects first in copper and brass. These are much less expensive than wire made of gold, sterling silver, or anodized niobium. "Anodizing" is a process of coloring metal by passing an electric current through a chemical bath which transfers a film of color to the surface of the metal.

Copper is a softer metal than brass and therefore easier to bend. You may want to experiment with copper wire before using brass. You'll also find that any thicker gauge wire will be slightly harder to bend than the thinner gauges.

Brass is an alloy of zinc and copper. High brass, which contains more zinc than copper, is a bright "brassy" yellow. Low brass, which contains more copper than zinc, has a mellow, reddish hue but is not as red as pure copper.

You will find copper and brass wire packaged in 1-pound (.5 kg) or 1/4-pound (112 g) spools. They are also packaged in smaller amounts in coils. Silver, purchased by the foot (centimeters, meters) or ounce (gram) is packaged in a coil.

Once you feel comfortable with the techniques in the book, you may want to use the more expensive wire or experiment with mixing metals within a project. The color photos of the finished projects (pages 33-40 and 57-64) give you an indication of some of the ways you can combine different metals for a variety of looks.

FINISHES

Once you complete a piece, you need to "finish" it. This can take several steps involving cleaning, polishing, oxidizing, or lacquering. The amount of finishing you do depends on the look you want for the piece. You can merely polish the metal with the jeweler's rouge, a gentle abrasive that brings out the shine and removes small nicks and tool marks, or you can apply an antiqued "oxidized" finish.

The natural process of oxygen acting on metal will "oxidize" it, turning the metal a darker shade. Once

metal has oxidized, you will need to polish it to restore its luster. By applying a finish to your projects, you can control the oxidation of the metal. By choosing either a clear or an oxidized (antique) finish, you're selecting the ultimate look for a piece.

Applying lacquer to a finished piece will inhibit oxidation. By doing this, you place a barrier between the metal and the air. If you want a bright look that shows the color of the metal, polish the piece after you make it and apply clear lacquer (you'll find instructions in Chapter One).

One of oldest and easiest ways to apply an antiqued finish is to dip the finished piece in a solution of liver of sulphur and water which darkens the metal.(Detailed instructions for this process are in Chapter One.) Then, using an abrasive material, you remove the color,

controlling the amount of highlights for the piece. You can leave as much or as little of the dark coloration as you want. This gives you many options in a range from a dark antiqued finish to lighter touches of shading that enhance the metal's natural color. Once you get the finish where you want it, apply the lacquer to seal the look.

There are also commercial preparations for creating oxidized finishes. You can find these in jewelry supply shops or through jewelry supply catalogs. Some of the substances are toxic, and we caution you to read the labels for any precautions you should take when using those products.

Do not apply lacquer to silver if you want a clear silver finish since the lacquer will dull the silver over time. It's better to polish silver occasionally to remove natural oxidation. If you are combining metals with silver in a project (see Mixing Metals below) lacquer the individual units made of copper and brass first before assembling the piece.

MIXING METALS

Pieces that are made of individual units, like the ones in this book, lend themselves to combining metals. You can create a variety of interesting looks for your projects by doing this. It's best to experiment to get an idea of how you can best utilize the shades of different metals to highlight a design.

Again, refer to the color photos of the finished projects (pages 33-40 and 57-64) to see how the designers have used mixed metals to enhance the designs.

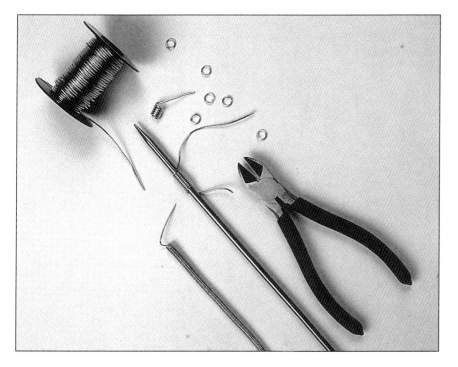

You can easily make jump rings and coils by using a knitting needle for a mandrel.

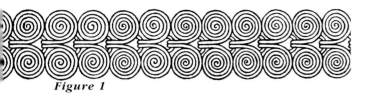

Figure 1

AN ANCIENT DESIGN

OVER FOUR THOUSAND YEARS AGO, an Egyptian goldsmith produced a lovely and unusual necklace made entirely of wire. As far as we know, he was the first designer to use the coil principle and the first to fit coiled links together in this ingenious fashion.

The basic idea seems to be one that occurred to expert metal workers of many times and places, for ornaments based on the same design have been found in the tombs of the rulers of such unrelated regions of the world as Persia and Peru.

Now it's your turn to practice this ancient technique as you create a coil bracelet.

MATERIALS

144 inches (3.6 m) of 20-gauge wire. A 1/4-pound (112 g) spool contains enough wire for three or four bracelets.

18-gauge wire. You will use only a few inches (centimeters),leaving enough to make several pieces described in later projects.

Fine steel wool

Liver of sulphur

Nonchlorine abrasive cleanser

Jeweler's rouge

Lacquer

Lacquer thinner

Wide-mouthed jar

TOOLS

Round-nosed pliers

Flat-nosed pliers or chain-nose, parallel pliers

#8 or #9 (US) knitting needles, or any hardwood stick or metal rod about 3/16 inch (5 mm) in diameter

Wire cutters

File

1" (2.5 cm) soft, natural-bristle brush

Hand buffer

1. Unwind about 8 inches (20.5 cm) of 20-gauge wire from the spool or coil. Always bend the wire away from the spool as shown in Figure 2. To avoid getting kinks in the wire, unwind it so it looks like Figure 3.

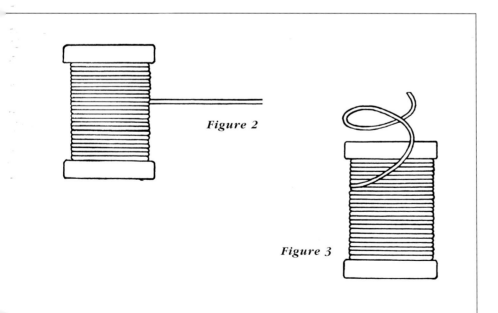

Figure 2

Figure 3

2. Cut 21 lengths of wire, each 6 1/2 inches (16.5 cm) long. Always cut one length of wire the correct size, and then measure the rest by it. Once they're cut, straighten the lengths of wire using your fingers rather than the pliers to avoid leaving tool marks (Figure 4).

3. Using the tip of the round-nosed pliers, curve both ends of each piece into a half-circle, and measure against Figure 5.

NOTE: A broken line in a drawing indicates that the illustration does not show the entire length of wire. Illustrations without a broken line are the actual size ("life-sized"), and you may use these as an exact model for measuring the wire.

4. Pinch the ends of each length of wire to look like Figure 7. If you have a pair of parallel pliers with a crosswise notch, use the notch to pinch the ends (Figure 6). Flat-nosed pliers may be used if you do not have parallel pliers.

NOTE: It may take a little practice before you are able to make the ends round instead of oval. Taking the time to make the ends round will result in a nicely rounded coil which is the desired look for this project.

5. Hold one end of one length in the flat-nosed or chain-nosed pliers, with the pliers in your right hand (Figure 8). (Every pair of pliers grips a little differently. Find the place in your pliers where they grip the best.) Then coil the end by pressing the wire up parallel with the edge of the pliers, using your left thumb (Figure 9).

6. Release the unit, then replace it in the pliers so that you can coil the wire farther around it (Figure 10). Continue in this manner. When the coil is large enough, use your right thumb and forefinger in place of the pliers (Figure 11).

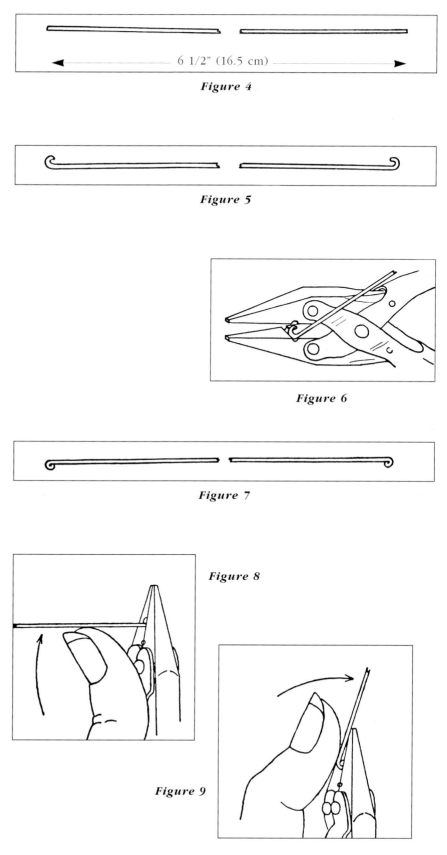

6 1/2" (16.5 cm)

Figure 4

Figure 5

Figure 6

Figure 7

Figure 8

Figure 9

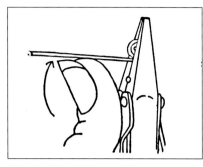

Figure 10

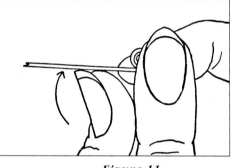

Figure 11

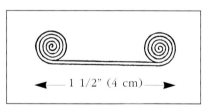

← 1 1/2" (4 cm) →

Figure 12

7. Stop coiling when the coil is approximately 1/4 inch (.5 cm) in diameter. Then coil the other end of the same length of wire (unit) toward the center in the same way. Stop coiling when this coil also measures 1/4 inch (.5 cm) in diameter.

8. Coil the ends of the unit alternately until the unit measures 1 1/2 inches (1.4 cm) overall, making the coils as near the same size as possible. Place the unit against Figure 12 to check the measurement and shape. If the unit is not quite flat, grasp the coils in your fingers and twist, so that they are both in the same plane. Repeat these steps on the other lengths of wire, and measure each one against Figure 12.

9. Hold the center point of one of the units in the tip of the round-nosed pliers. Bend both coils back towards the center and toward each other, using the thumb and forefinger of your left hand (Figure 13). If you see that one side is going to be longer than the other, release the shorter side and bend the longer one until they are even and the unit looks like Figure 14. Repeat these steps on the other units.

10. To flatten and stiffen the units, first lay several layers of newspaper on a sturdy table. Place one unit on top of the newspaper. Pound the unit, using a small rubber mallet or the heel of a shoe. Do not use a hammer with a metal head, even if it's been padded, since this will mark the wire. Repeat these steps with each of the other units.

11. Hold one unit in the flat-nosed or parallel pliers in your right hand, so that the edge of the pliers is in line with the top of the coils (Figure 15). Then bend the coils downward sharply to form a right angle, using your left thumb. The unit will now look like Figure 16. Repeat these steps on the other units.

12. Using your fingers, pinch the loop of one of the units down flat to the coils. It should look like Figure 17 which shows the outside of the unit, and Figure 18 which shows the inside. Next, hold the same unit, outside up, in your left hand. Insert the loop of another unit down through the loop of the first unit (Figure 19). Pinch the second unit until it too is flat (Figure 20). Assemble the remaining units in the same manner. Add or subtract units if the bracelet is too short or too long. Twenty-one units, plus the clasp (which adds about 1/2 inch (1.5 cm)) are enough for the average wrist.

13. To make the hook, cut one length of 20-gauge wire 7 1/2 inches (19 cm) long. Coil this length from each end following Steps 3-8 for making the other units. Stop coiling when the hook unit is 2 1/2

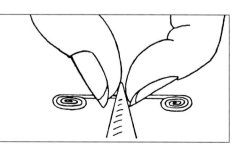

Figure 13

Figure 14

Figure 15

Figure 16

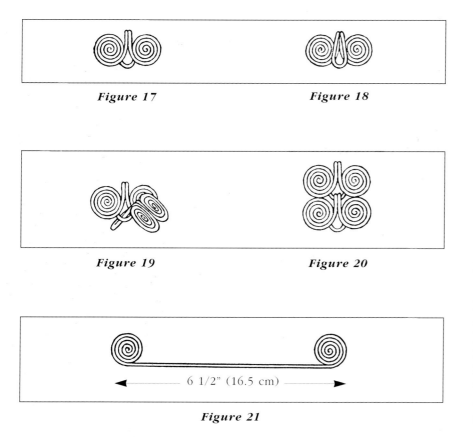

Figure 17   Figure 18

Figure 19   Figure 20

6 1/2" (16.5 cm)

Figure 21

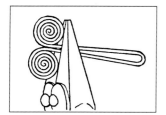

Figure 22

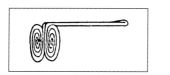

Figure 23

Figure 24   Figure 25

inches (6.5 cm) overall, measuring it against Figure 21.

14. Hold the center point of the unit in the tip of the round-nosed pliers. Bend both coils back toward the center (and toward each other) using the thumb and forefinger of your left hand. Hold the unit in the parallel or flat-nosed pliers in your right hand, so the edge of the pliers is in line with the tops of the coils (Figure 22). Bend the coils downward at a right angle. This will leave a much longer loop for bending the hook (Figure 23).

15. Insert the loop down through the loop of the last unit of the assembled bracelet. Flatten this unit, using your fingers. Pinch the sides of the loop as close together as possible, using the parallel or

flat-nosed pliers (Figure 24). Bend the loop back against the inside of the bracelet, using the round-nosed pliers to make a hook (Figure 25).

JUMP RINGS

The following steps will show you how to make a "jump ring" to be used as an eye for the hook. These instructions will help you learn the correct way to wind wire on a mandrel for making jump rings, chain units, and coils for other projects in the book.

16. Wrap 18-gauge wire around the knitting needle or stick. Hold the end of the wire and the stick in your left hand. Keep the spool, coil, or length of wire close to the stick or knitting needle as you wind the wire tightly onto it. Keep the rounds of wire as close to each other and as even and straight as you can.

Like this:

Not like this:

Not like this:

17. Remove the spring you've just formed from the knitting needle, and trim the ends. Using the wire cutters, cut one complete round from the spring (Figure 29). This round is called a "jump ring."

Figure 31

Figure 32

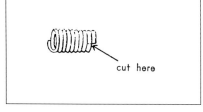

Figure 29

Figure 30

Figure 33

Figure 34

18. Using the parallel or flat-nosed pliers and your fingers, open the jump ring. *Always open a jump ring sideways, as shown in Figure 30. Never pull it wide as shown in Figure 31.*

19. Using the file, file the ends of the ring flat, removing the burr (Figure 32). A file, like a saw, has teeth, all of which point away from its handle. Therefore, in order to file efficiently and save the teeth of the file, you must always file forward, never back and forth.

20. Slip the jump ring through the bent-over loop of the first unit of the assembled bracelet (Figure 33). Close the jump ring, using the parallel or flat-nosed pliers and your fingers. *In closing a jump ring, always push one end a little past the other, as shown in Figure 34, and then push it back in line. This puts a bit of spring into it and makes it hold better.* Turn the jump ring so that the joint is inside

the first unit. Save the rest of the spring. You will use more jump rings later for other bracelets and necklaces.

FINISHING

The following steps will take you through the basics of how to finish the metal for an antiqued look. This process is called "oxidizing," and its purpose is to add color to the piece of jewelry, emphasize its design, and remove the new, raw look from the metal.

The liver of sulphur oxidizes the metal, turning it dark. The use of an abrasive material (here, the nonchlorine abrasive cleanser) allows you to bring back the original color of the metal where you want it, giving you control over the amount of antiquing for the piece.

If you do not want an antique finish and prefer letting the original

color of the metal show through, follow Step 21 then Steps 25-30. This will provide a clear, protective finish and will help retard the natural oxidation of the metal that takes place over time.

You can use spray lacquer. However, the dipped finish as described below will give you optimum results. When using spray lacquer, apply several light coats, allowing each coat to dry thoroughly before applying the next one.

21. Scrub the bracelet if it has become discolored or dirty, using the soft, 1-inch (2.5 cm), natural-bristle brush. Then rinse and dry the bracelet with a clean cloth.

22. Dip the bracelet into a solution made with one-half cup warm water and enough liver of sulphur to turn the water dark brown. Then rinse the bracelet in cold water to remove the excess black.

NOTE: You will need a piece of liver of sulphur about the size of a lump of sugar. This solution will keep only three or four weeks without deteriorating. It is best to store it in a dark area. It is no longer usable when it has a scum on its surface or a sediment in it.

23. Wet your thumb and dip it into the cleanser. Rub the bracelet with your thumb (which is really the most efficient instrument for reaching the hidden spots) or with a homemade buffer with cleanser on it (if your thumb gets too tired) until the highlights are clean. The amount of black you remove depends on your personal taste.

24. Rinse the bracelet in warm water, using a brush to remove all the cleanser. This is very important. Then dry the bracelet thoroughly.

25. Polish the bracelet with the hand buffer on which you have rubbed some jeweler's rouge. Replenish the rouge on the buffer only as necessary to achieve a high polish without covering the bracelet with excess rouge. Never use the same buffer for cleanser and rouge.

26. Scrub the bracelet back and front with soap and very hot water, using the soft, natural-bristle brush to remove the rouge completely. Rinse and dry the bracelet carefully. It must be absolutely clean at this point. Lacquer will just slide off metal that is wet or dirty.

NOTE: If you are using silver wire, your bracelet is now finished. It is not advisable to lacquer silver. Even the best lacquer yellows a bit with time, and while this does not matter with copper, it makes silver look as though it has been dipped in glue.

27. Pour approximately two parts of lacquer thinner to one part lacquer into a wide-mouthed

jar with a screw top. The mixture should be of an almost watery consistency. The lacquer may be thin enough to use right from the can when you first buy it, but it will thicken over time. If you are using old lacquer from around the house, it will usually be much too thick by the time you use it and must be thinned with the lacquer thinner.

28. Make a hook in the end of a piece of wire (any gauge will do).

Pick up the bracelet by catching the hook through the jump ring so that the bracelet hangs free. Dip the whole bracelet into the lacquer for a few seconds. Remove the excess lacquer, using a toothpick to lead off whatever drops form as the bracelet hangs free. Also, puncture any "window panes" of lacquer that form between units or in loops.

29. Hang the bracelet to dry where it can hang free and where there is as little dampness and dust as possible. Since metal "sweats," it is not satisfactory to lacquer on a hot, damp day.

30. Repeat the dipping of the bracelet into the lacquer no sooner than four hours later. Two thin coats of lacquer are far better than one heavy coat. Hang the bracelet to dry for at least 12 hours. Jeweler's lacquer, if applied correctly, will keep copper from turning dark for an indefinite length of time.

NOTE: In time, lacquer may flake off. You may choose to not lacquer the metal, allowing natural oxidation to occur. You can remove this oxidation with a polishing cloth that you can purchase at a jewelry store, or you can restore the piece by gently cleaning it with the nonchlorine abrasive cleanser,

then polishing it using the jeweler's rouge and hand buffer following Steps 25 and 26.

HOW TO MAKE A MATCHING NECKLACE

Use the same materials and tools used for the bracelet (see page 12). You will use 280 inches (7 m) of 20-gauge wire and about 1 inch (2.5 cm) of 18-gauge wire.

1. Cut 42 lengths of 20-gauge wire, each 6 1/2 inches (16.5 cm) long.

2. Make and assemble the 42 links, or units, according to the directions for the bracelet in Steps 3-12. Add or subtract units if the necklace is not the proper size. Allow 1/2 inch (1.5 cm) to be taken up by the clasp.

3. Make and attach a hook on one end as described in Steps 13-15. Cut another jump ring from the spring you have saved from Step 17, and attach it on the other end.

4. Apply a finish to the necklace by following the instructions for finishing the bracelet in Steps 21-30.

Figure 35

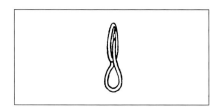

Figure 36

HOW TO MAKE MATCHING EARRINGS

Use the same materials and tools you used for the bracelet, plus some household cement and a pair of commercial earring backs or French wires. You will need 46 inches (1.1 m) of 20-gauge wire.

1. Cut two lengths of 20-gauge wire each 5 inches (12.5 cm) long; two lengths 5 1/2 inches (14 cm) long; two lengths 6 inches (15 cm) long; and two lengths 6 1/2 inches (16.5 cm) long.

2. Coil one end of each of the 5-inch (12.5 cm) lengths until you have 1 inch (2.5 cm) left at the end of each unit.

3. Using the round-nosed pliers, curve the 1-inch (2.5 cm) end into a loop like the one on the top unit in Figure 35, then press the end against the back of the coil, so that from the side the unit looks like Figure 36 .

4. Coil the ends of each of the other lengths toward each other as you did the bracelet units. Stop coiling when the 5 1/2-inch (14 cm) lengths measure 1 inch (2.5 cm) and the coils are the same size. The 6-inch (15 cm) lengths

will measure 1 1/4 inches (3 cm) when coiled. The 6 1/2-inch (16.5 cm) lengths will measure 1 1/2 inches (4 cm) like the bracelet units (see Figure 12).

5. Bend the coils of each of these units toward each other as you did the bracelet units (see Figures 13 and 14).

6. Open the loops on the back of the first units sideways, using the parallel or flat-nosed pliers just as you did when you opened the jump ring.

7. Assemble the earrings as shown in Figure 35, and apply a finish according to the directions in Steps 21-30.

8. Attach a commercial earring back to the top unit of each earring. Use household cement or liquid solder which you can find in craft supply shops or hardware stores.

NOTE: You may find a clamp useful to hold the coil and the back tightly together while they're drying. You can make one very easily by cutting a piece of heavy-gauge wire and bending it into whatever shape is suitable. For instance, you might make a clamp like Figure 37, from 14-gauge wire

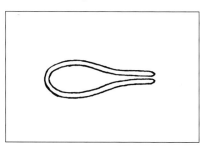

Figure 37

EARRINGS WITH FRENCH WIRES

You can also make earrings using commercial French wires as shown in the color photo on page 33. (These wires already had the antiqued copper bead on them when purchased.)

1. Cut two lengths of 20-gauge wire 5 1/2 inches (14 cm) long; two lengths 6 inches (15 cm) long; and two lengths 6 1/2 inches (16.5 cm) long.

2. Coil the ends of each of the other lengths toward each other as you did the bracelet units. Stop coiling when the 5 1/2-inch (14 cm) lengths measure 1 inch (2.5 cm) and the coils are the same size. The 6-inch (15 cm) lengths will measure 1 1/4 inches (3 cm) when coiled. The 6 1/2-inch (16.5 cm) lengths will measure 1 1/2 inches (4 cm) as in Figure 12.

3. Bend the coils of each of these units toward each other as you did the bracelet units (see Figures 13 and 14). Assemble the three units as shown in Figure 35, and apply a finish according to the directions in Steps 21-30.

4. Attach a commercial French wire to the loop of the top unit.

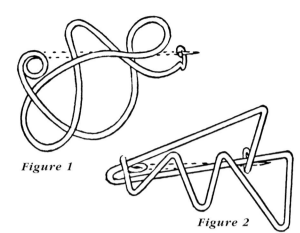

Figure 1

Figure 2

EXPERIMENTING WITH HEAVIER WIRE

THIS IS YOUR FIRST MEETING WITH heavy-gauge wire. You will soon learn that it has a mind of its own. Having been drawn through a draw plate, wire has direction or intention; there are things it wants to do and things it doesn't want to do. For instance, wire will not stand being bent back and forth too many times in the same place. This produces friction that makes the wire so brittle it finally breaks.

Do not torture wire. All wire has a natural curve in it. Therefore, when making a curving design, bend it in the direction it wants to go. Experimentation will teach you to take advantage of its natural tendencies and how to avoid being rough which causes ugly distortions.

The lapel pins in Figures 1 and 2 were first made in this manner, letting the wire help with creating the design. If you prefer, by following the general principles given here, let your own piece of wire help you to design something a bit different from the pins shown.

HOW TO MAKE THE LAPEL PIN IN FIGURE 1

MATERIALS

12 1/2 inches (31.5 cm) of 14-gauge wire

Steel wool

Nonchlorine abrasive cleanser

Newspaper

Liver of sulphur

Rouge on a buffer

Lacquer

Lacquer thinner

TOOLS

Wire cutters

Round-nosed pliers NOTE: Use these as little as possible. In this case, fingers are better tools.

Mallet

1. Cut a piece of 14-gauge wire 12 1/2 inches (31.5 cm) long.

File one end round. To make a smooth, rounded surface, file for-ward in a curved plane, turning the wire at each stroke, as in Figure 3.

2. Using your fingers, bend the wire to make a right angle about 3/4 inch (2 cm) from the rounded end (Point A in figure 4). This end will later become the hook; meanwhile, it gives you something to hold onto while you manipulate the rest of the wire.

3. Using your fingers, curve the wire to fit Figure 4.

4. Loop the wire back over itself as shown in Figure 5, and then continue to bend it, using your fingers all the time, to fit Figures 6 and 7. Keep measuring against the drawings as you progress. Make sure you cross the wire over or under itself just as in the figures.

5. Place the unit on several layers of paper, and pound it as you did for the projects in Chapter One.

6. Using the round-nosed pliers, bend the 3/4-inch (2 cm) end into a hook as shown in the side view of the pin in Figure 8 at Point A.

7. Wrap the other end around the round-nosed pliers to form a spring

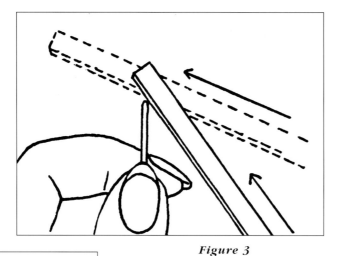

Figure 3

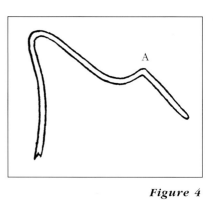

Figure 4

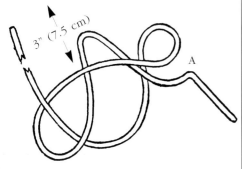

Figure 5

as shown in Figure 8 at Point B. This spring is just like the one on a safety pin except here it is allowed to show as part of the design.

8. Straighten the long end, which will make the "pin tong" (the part that pins). File the tong to a long, tapered point, and smooth it carefully, first using steel wool and then abrasive cleanser.

9. Place the tong on several layers of newspaper. Using the mallet, pound the tong to make it very hard.

10. Apply a finish according to the directions in Chapter One, Steps 21-30.

HOW TO MAKE THE PIN IN FIGURE 2

Use the same materials and tools you used for the first pin with the addition of the parallel or flat-nosed pliers.

1. Cut a piece of 14-gauge wire 20 inches (51 cm) long.

File one end round just as you did with the first pin.

2. Bend the wire to make an angle 3/4 inch (2 cm) from the rounded end. This pin is made with sharp angles, so you will use the parallel or flat-nosed pliers as well as your fingers. The easiest way to make a

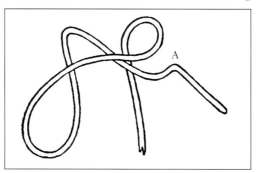

Figure 6

Figure 7

Figure 8

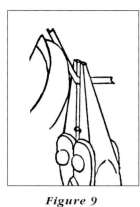

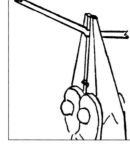

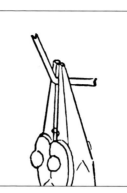

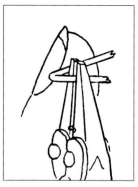

| Figure 9 | Figure 10 | Figure 11 | Figure 12 |

sharp angle is to first bend the wire against the side of the pliers (Figure 9). Next, without letting go, pull it back (Figure 10). Then bend it again in the same place (Figure 11). When you have done this, you can bend an acute angle very easily with your fingers (Figure 12).

3. Bend the wire to fit Figures 13, 14, and 15 in turn.

4. Place the unit on several layers of paper and pound it as you did the first pin.

5. Using the round-nosed pliers, bend the 3/4-inch (2 cm) end into a hook as shown in Figure 16 at Point A. Then wrap the other end around the round-nosed pliers to form a spring as shown in Figure 16 at Point B.

6. Straighten the long end for the pin tong. Use the file, steel wool, and abrasive cleanser on the end of the pin tong. Then, pound the pin tong until it is hard as you did for the first pin.

7. Apply a finish according to the directions in Chapter One, Steps 21-30.

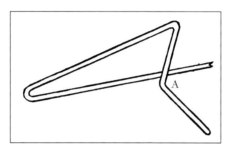

Figure 13

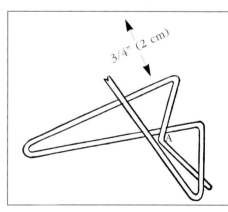

Figure 14

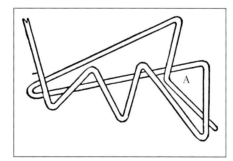

Figure 15

Figure 16

Figure 1

A SIMPLE CHAIN

A "MANDREL" IS ANYTHING USED as a core around which wire is bent to make a spring of a given size and shape. It can be a knitting needle, a nail, or a pen. Mandrels do not always have to be round. Wooden dowels for instance, can be whittled to make mandrels that are oval, square, rectangular, tapering, and so on. You have already used a mandrel to make jump rings.

We've found that metal knitting needles make the best round mandrels. They're strong, come in a range of sizes based on their diameters, and are easily found in general merchandise stores.

The chain illustrated in Figure 1 is made on a mandrel.

You'll find this chain easy to make and its classic design easy to wear.

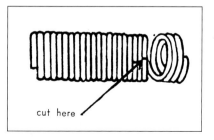

cut here

Figure 2

TO MAKE A BRACELET OF THIS CHAIN

MATERIALS

115 inches (2.8 m) of 16-gauge wire

4 1/4 inches (11 cm) of 14-gauge wire

Liver of sulphur

Nonchlorine abrasive cleanser

Jeweler's rouge

Lacquer

Lacquer thinner

TOOLS

Parallel pliers or flat-nosed pliers

Round-nosed pliers

A mandrel about 3/8 inch (1 cm) in diameter, the approximate size of a #15 or #16 (US) knitting needle.

1. Wind 16-gauge wire around the mandrel. Check the directions and drawings on page 15 for the correct way to do this. Stop winding when you have made 88 complete rounds of wire.

2. Remove the spring you've made from the mandrel, cut it free from the spool or coil, and trim the ends.

3. Bend a unit of four rounds away from the end of the spring and cut it free as illustrated in Figure 2. Continue bending and cutting until you have 22 units of four rounds each.

4. File both ends of each unit to remove the burr so that there will be no roughness to catch on clothing. Remember to file forward rather than back and forth.

5. Hold one unit in each hand. Insert the end of the unit that is in your right hand (B in the figures below) down through the center of the other unit (A). Wind unit B through unit A. Watch to see that the end of B always passes inside of A as you wind, and be sure always to keep winding in the same direction.

6. Assemble the rest of the units by winding each one onto the preceding unit to make a chain. The winding will spread the rounds apart. Pinch each unit after it has been wound onto the chain so the rounds will lie close together.

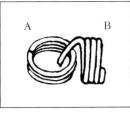

Figure 3

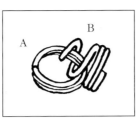

Figure 4

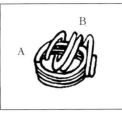

Figure 5

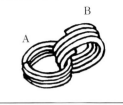

Figure 6

7. Grasp one end of the first unit in the tip of the round-nosed pliers, as shown in Figure 7. Bend the end so that it is hidden close inside the unit. Figure 8 shows how the finished unit should look from the side, and Figure 9 shows how it should look from the top. Do not let the end protrude into the center of the unit, but make sure the end unit looks like Figure 9, rather than Figure 10.

Bend each end of each unit in the same way.

8. Make a jump ring by winding a 14-gauge wire around the mandrel several times. Then cut a jump ring from this spring. It is always easier to make a spring long enough for several jump rings since you can always use the extra ones later.

9. Open the jump ring sideways. File both ends of the jump ring flat and smooth.

10. Using the parallel pliers or flat-nosed pliers and your fingers, insert the open jump ring through the end unit of the chain and close it (see Figure 13).

11. Cut one 2 3/4-inch (7 cm) length of 14-gauge wire to make the hook. File one end of the 2 3/4-inch (7 cm) length flat, the other round. Bend the flat end around the base of the round-nosed pliers to form a loop with an inside diameter of about 3/8 inch (1 cm) (Figure 11). Always make loops round, never oval, unless the directions specifically say so.

12. Using the round-nosed pliers, bend the other end into a hook (Figure 12), Open the loop sideways, using the parallel pliers. *A loop should be opened sideways just as you open a jump ring.* Insert the open loop through the unit at the other end of the chain from the jump ring and close the loop (figure 13).

13. Apply a finish according to the directions in Chapter One, Steps 21-30.

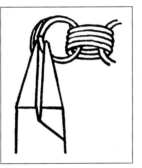

Figure 7

Figure 8

Figure 9

Figure 10

Figure 11

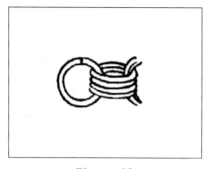

Figure 13

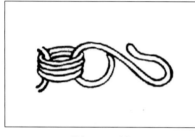

Figure 12

Figure 14

HOW TO MAKE A MATCHING NECKLACE

YOU WILL NEED:

262 inches (6.5 m) of 16-gauge wire

3 1/2 inches (9 cm) of 14-gauge wire

The same mandrel you used for the bracelet.

The rest of the same tools and materials you used for the bracelet.

1. Wind 200 rounds of 16-gauge wire around the mandrel.

2. Cut 50 units of four rounds each from the spring.

3. Make and assemble the units in the same way you made the chain for the bracelet.

4. Make and attach a hook and jump ring like the ones you made for the bracelet.

5. Apply a finish according to the directions in Chapter One, Steps 21-30.

HOW TO MAKE MATCHING EARRINGS

YOU WILL NEED:

53 inches (1.3 m) of 18-gauge wire

A mandrel about 5/16 of an inch (8 mm) in diameter, the approximate size of a #13 (US) knitting needle.

The rest of the same tools and materials you used for making the bracelet and necklace.

1. Wind 48 rounds of 18-gauge wire around the mandrel.

2. Cut 12 units of four rounds each from the spring.

3. Make two chains of six units each, like the chain you made for the bracelet.

4. Wind the sixth unit of each chain through the first unit (Figure 15).

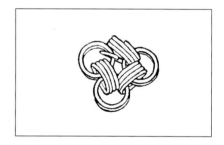

Figure 15

5. Turn each unit of each earring so that the ends are hidden inside where they will not catch on the wearer's hair.

6. Apply a finish according to the directions in "An Ancient Design," Steps 21-30.

7. Attach commercial earring backs according to the directions in Chapter One, Step 8. You can also attach French wires for dangle earrings.

Figure 1

TWO SIZES OF WIRE

4
CHAPTER

THIS NECKLACE WAS DESIGNED especially for a plain, round neckline. The combination of two weights of wire creates two contrasting textures. Some people find this design more pleasing than the previous project, "A Simple Chain." Perhaps you'll find the variety an enjoyable change as you work.

MATERIALS

80 inches (2 m) of 18-gauge wire

30 1/2 inches (77.5 cm) of 14-gauge wire

Liver of sulphur

Nonchlorine abrasive cleanser

Jeweler's rouge

Lacquer

Lacquer Thinner

TOOLS

Round-nosed pliers

Parallel pliers or flat-nosed pliers

File

Mandrel about 5/32 inch (3.75mm) in diameter, the approximate size of a #5 (US) knitting needle

Hand buffer

1. Cut 11 lengths of 14-gauge wire, each 3 inches (7 cm) long.

File all the ends round and smooth. Remember to file forward, never back and forth. Figure 3, on page 20, shows how to file wire round.

2. Using the round-nosed pliers, loop both ends of each length of wire. Make a loop that is round, not oval, by holding the wire and pliers as shown in Figure 11 of the previous project, "A Simple Chain". Figure 2 shows the exact size of the loops.

3. With your fingers, gently curve each unit in the center.

Measure each one against Figure 2.

4. Wind 18-gauge wire around the mandrel (#5 (US) knitting needle) using the techniques in Chapter One. Stop winding when you have made 129 complete rounds of wire. Remove the spring formed by the rounds of wire from the mandrel, cut it free from the spool, and trim the ends.

5. Cut nine units of nine rounds of wire from the mandrel, cut it free from the spool, and trim the ends.

6. Slide the tip of the parallel or flat-nosed pliers around between

Figure 2

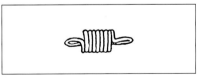

Figure 3

Figure 4

Figure 5

the first two rounds of one of the units, until one round is bent away from the rest. Grip that round in the pliers, and twist it sideways so that it lies across the end opening of the unit, as shown in Figures 3 and 4. Open both end rounds of each unit in the same way. Bend each nine-round unit in the center, using your fingers. Each one should now fit Figure 5.

7. For the hook, cut one piece of 14-gauge wire 2 inches (5 cm) long.

File one end flat, the other round. Loop the flat end.

Make a hook on the other end like this:

Figure 6

8. Cut a jump ring from the spring you made for Chapter Three

(16-gauge wire wound around a #15 or #16 (US) knitting needle). Open the jump ring, using the parallel pliers and your fingers, remembering that jump rings and loops must always be opened sideways. File the ends of the jump ring flat.

9. Using the parallel or flat-nosed pliers, open the loops of all the 18-gauge units sideways.

10. Assemble the necklace units in the order shown in Figure 1. Close the loops of the 18-gauge units.

11. Attach the hook to the right-hand end, the jump ring to the other. Push the ends of the 18-gauge units against the inside of the spring so that they will not catch on clothing.

12. Apply a finish of your choice as explained in Chapter One.

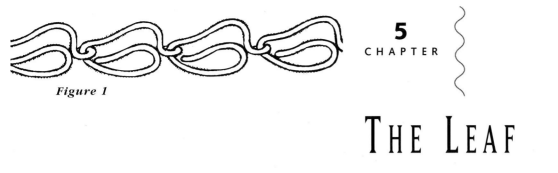

Figure 1

THE LEAF

ALTHOUGH THIS DESIGN IS EASY to follow, it will help you now and with future designs to understand the following explanation of bending as illustrated in Figures 2, 3, and 4.

In Figure 2, the pliers grip a 4-inch (10 cm) length of wire exactly in the center.

In Figure 3, the left end of the wire, marked A, has been bent completely around the base of the pliers. This end is now 1/22 inch (1 mm) shorter than the other.

In Figure 4, the right end, marked B, has been bent in the same way, making it shorter.

When you're following directions for bending, try to bend both ends equally unless the drawing indicates that one end is meant to come out longer than the other. A little practice will sharpen your judgment.

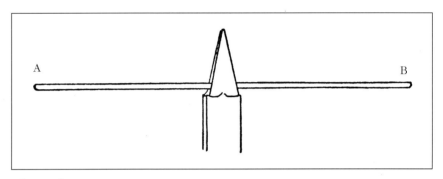

Figure 2

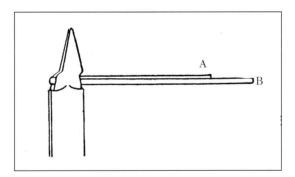

Figure 3

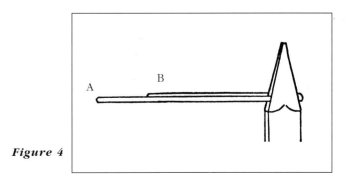

Figure 4

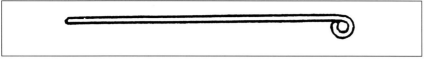

Figure 5

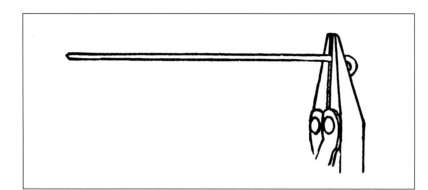

Figure 6

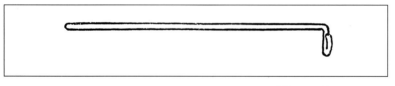

Figure 7

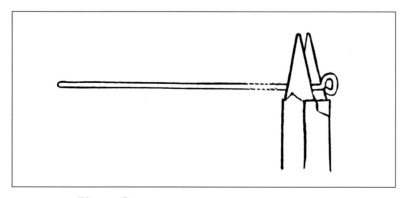

Figure 8

HOW TO MAKE A LEAF BRACELET

MATERIALS

26 inches (66 cm) of 14-gauge wire

Liver of sulphur

Nonchlorine abrasive cleanser

Jeweler's rouge

Lacquer

Lacquer Thinner

TOOLS

Round-nosed pliers

Parallel pliers or flat-nosed pliers

File

Hand buffer

1. Cut seven lengths of 14-gauge wire, each 3 1/2 inches (9 cm) long. File one end of each length round, the other flat.

2. Using the round-nosed pliers, loop the flat end of each length, and measure each one against Figure 5.

3. Hold the loop of one of the lengths in the parallel or flat-nosed pliers, as shown in Figure 6. Press the wire away from you, using your left thumb, so that it lies against the side of the pliers. Repeat this operation on each unit, measuring each one against Figure 7.

4. Hold one of the units in the round-nosed pliers with the long end of the wire pointing away from you as shown in Figure 8.

5. Bend the wire *toward* you to produce the curve lettered A in Figure 9, and then press the wire against your left forefinger to make the curve lettered B in Figure 9.

Repeat these steps on the other units, measuring each one against Figure 9 as you complete the two curves.

6. Hold one of the units in the tip of the round-nosed pliers, placing the pliers at a point just beyond Curve B. Bend the wire sharply back around the pliers to form the curve shown in Figure 10. Curve the other units in the same way, measuring each one against Figure 10 as you complete it.

7. Using your fingers, bend each unit to fit Figure 11.

8. Using the round-nosed pliers, bend each unit to fit Figure 12, then Figure 13.

9. For the hook, cut a piece of 14-gauge wire 1 1/2 inches (4 cm) long.

File one end of the piece flat, the other end round. Loop the flat end, making a hook as shown in Figure 14.

10. Open the loops of the leaf units and of the hook sideways.

Assemble the bracelet by inserting the opened loop of each unit through the tip of the next unit as shown in Figure 1, and closing the loop.

11. Apply a finish of your choice.

HOW TO MAKE A NECKLACE OF THIS DESIGN

YOU WILL NEED:

61 1/2 (1.5 cm) inches of 14-gauge wire

The rest of the same tools and materials you used for the bracelet.

1. Cut 15 lengths of 14-gauge wire, each 4 inches (10 cm) long.

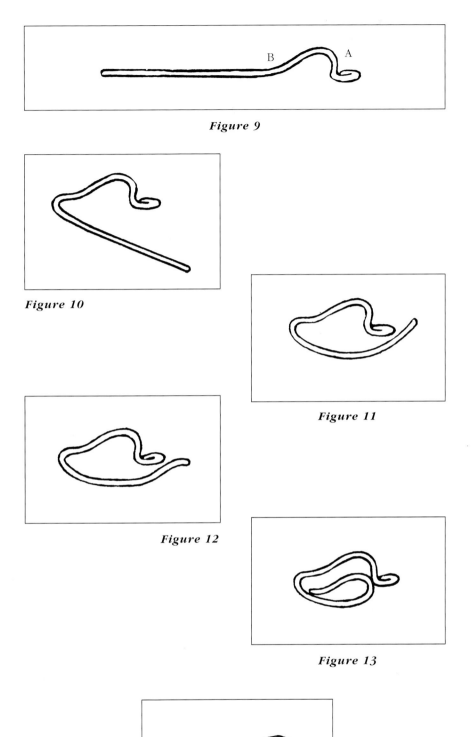

Figure 9

Figure 10

Figure 11

Figure 12

Figure 13

Figure 14

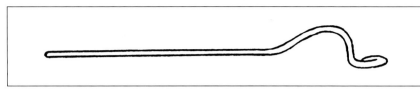

Figure 15

Figure 16

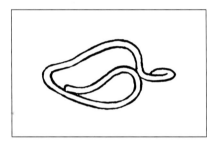

Figure 17

File one end of each length flat, the other round.

2. Bend each unit into the same leaf shape you made for the bracelet, following the same steps but measuring each unit against the drawings below (Figures 15, 16, and 17) as it reaches the appropriate stage.

3. Using the parallel pliers or flat-nosed pliers, bend the loop of

each unit more sharply than the original right angle. This makes the necklace curve more gracefully around the neck.

4. Cut a piece of 14-gauge wire 1 1/2 (4 cm) inches long to make the hook. File one end flat, the other end round. Make a hook like the one you made for the bracelet (Figure 14).

5. Assemble the necklace in the same way that you assembled the bracelet.

6. Apply a finish of your choice.

HOW TO MAKE SLIP-ON EARRINGS OF THIS DESIGN

These earrings are very practical and comfortable to wear if they are fitted just right. They are especially nice for women who wear their hair short or up in the back and are not happy with the way the usual earring backs look from behind. If the wearer finds a pair of these slip-on earrings too tight or too loose, they may be bent at the center curve so that the sides are closer together or farther apart. The sides *must* be parallel.

YOU WILL NEED:

12 inches (30.5 cm) of 14-gauge wire

The same tools and materials you used for the bracelet.

1. Cut two lengths of 14-gauge wire, each 6 inches (15 cm) long.

File all the ends round.

2. Using the round-nosed pliers and your fingers, bend each length to fit Figure 19.

3. Bend each unit at the center point marked A in Figure 19 to make an earring like the one shown in Figure 18. Be sure to keep each leaf shape flat and level or the earring will pinch wherever it is uneven. The reason this earring is so comfortable is that the pressure is distributed over the whole area and not at just one point.

4. Apply a finish of your choice.

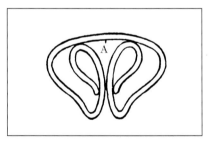

Figure 19

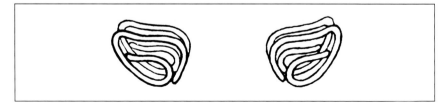

Figure 18

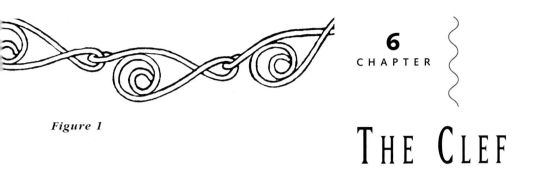

Figure 1

THE CLEF

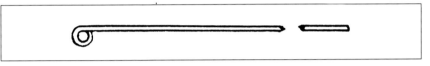

Figure 2

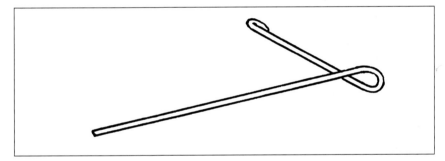

Figure 3

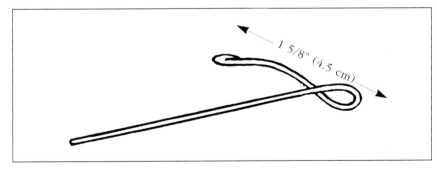

Figure 4

WE CALL THIS PROJECT THE CLEF because many people have told us this design reminds them of that musical symbol.

NOTE: From now on we will assume that you have all the necessary tools and materials for making the projects. Therefore, we will no longer list them at the beginning of each project with the exception of telling you the size and amount of wire to use as well as the size mandrel to use when necessary.

YOU WILL NEED:

---

64 1/2 inches (1.6 m) of 14-gauge wire

1. Cut 11 lengths of 14-gauge wire, each 5 1/2 inches (14 cm) long.

File one end of each length flat, the other end round.

2. Loop the flat end of each length to fit Figure 2. Hold one of the units in the round-nosed pliers, at a point 1 5/8 inches (4.2 cm) from the looped end.

3. Make a larger loop, then measure the unit against Figure 3. Repeat this operation on the other units, measuring each one against Figure 3.

4. Using your fingers, bend the looped end of each unit to fit Figure 4.

5. Loop the other end of each unit around the base of the round-nosed pliers, so that it fits Figure 5.

6. Using your fingers or pliers or both, whichever you find easiest, roll the larger loop of each unit, measuring each unit against Figure 6.

7. Hold one of the units as shown in Figure 7. Press your thumbs to

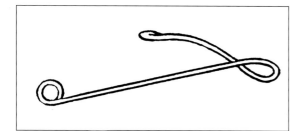

Figure 5

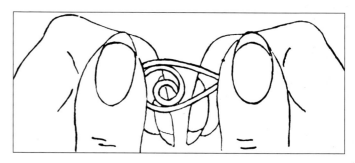

Figure 7

Figure 6

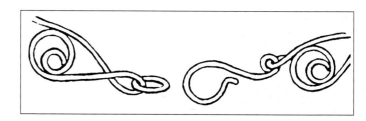

Figure 8

bend the unit so that it curves slightly away from you at each end. Then shift your left thumb, and press the coiled loop so that it lies a bit behind the top part of the unit. Bend each unit in the same manner. This step makes the necklace lie more gracefully.

8. Cut a jump ring from the spring you made for Chapter Three. (If you do not have one left, see page 22.) Open the jump ring sideways. File the ends of the jump ring flat.

9. For the hook, cut one 2 1/2-inch (6.5 cm) length of 14-gauge wire. File one end flat, the other end round. Using the round-nosed pliers, make a hook on the rounded end.

10. Open all loops, and assemble the necklace as shown in Figure 1. As shown in Figure 8, attach the hook, then attach the jump ring on the other end.

11. Apply a finish of your choice.

HOW TO MAKE SLIP-ON EARRINGS OF THIS DESIGN

YOU WILL NEED:

18 inches (45.5 cm) of 14-gauge wire

1. Cut two lengths of 14-gauge wire, each 9 inches (23 cm) long.

File all the ends round.

2. Using the round-nosed pliers, bend each length to fit Figure 10.

Then bend each unit at the point marked A in figure 10 to produce an earring like the ones shown in Figure 9. Do not bend these units in your fingers after they are formed the way you bent the necklace units because each side must be flat and parallel to the other side if the earrings are to be comfortable to wear.

3. Apply a finish of your choice.

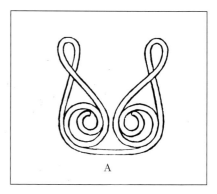

Figure 9

Figure 10

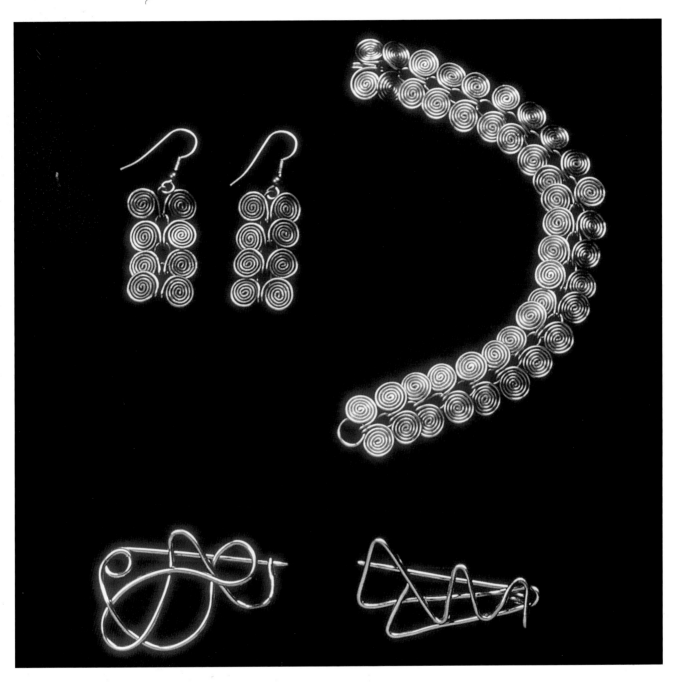

Top: *Chapter One, "An Ancient Design." Copper earrings in an antiqued finish with French wires; copper bracelet with a clear finish.*

Bottom: *Chapter Two, "Experimenting With Heavier Wire." (left) Lapel pin of copper with clear finish; (right) lapel pin of brass with clear finish.*

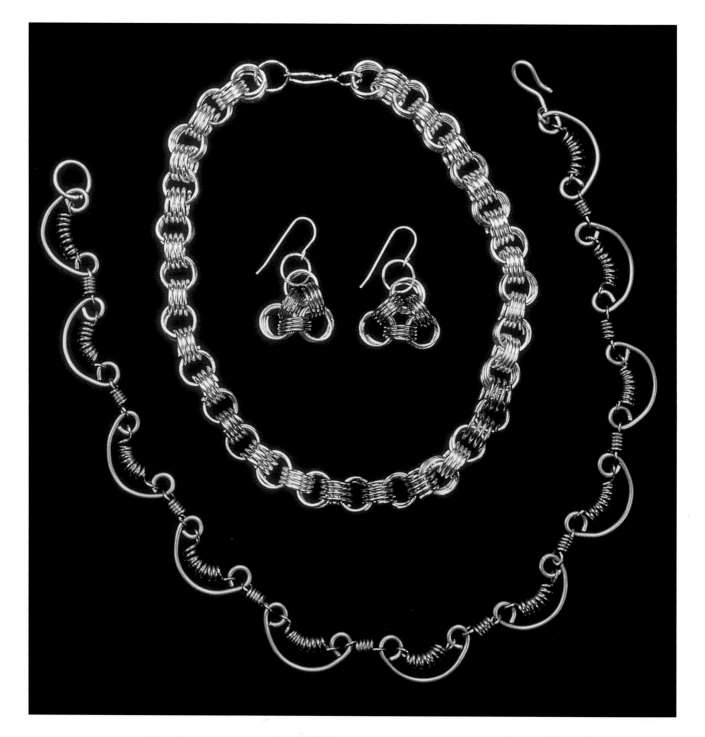

Top:
Chapter Three, "A Simple Chain." Necklace of sterling silver and copper with clear finish; earrings of sterling silver and copper with French wires.

Bottom:
Chapter Four, "Two Sizes of Wire." Necklace of low brass and copper with clear finish.

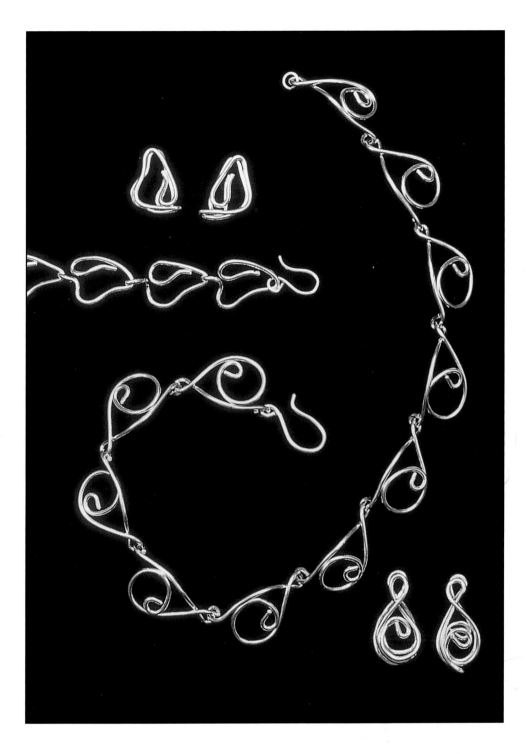

Clockwise:
Chapter Five,
"The Leaf."
Bracelet and
slip-on earrings of
sterling silver;

Chapter Six,
"The Clef."
Necklace and
slip-on earrings of
sterling silver.

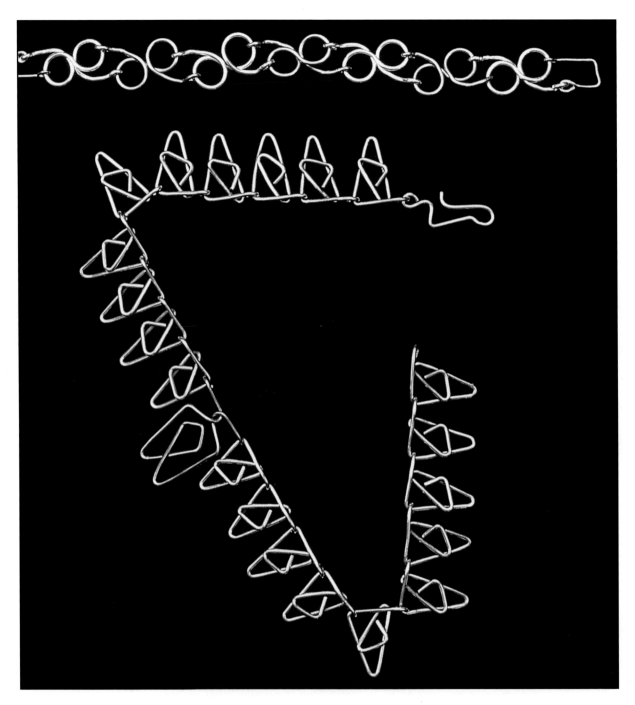

Top:
Chapter Seven,
"Figure Eights."
Bracelet of
sterling silver and
copper.

Bottom:
Chapter Eight,
"All Angles."
Necklace of low brass
and cooper.
The central unit is

cooper with an
antiqued finish, the
necklace units are
of low brass with a
clear finish.

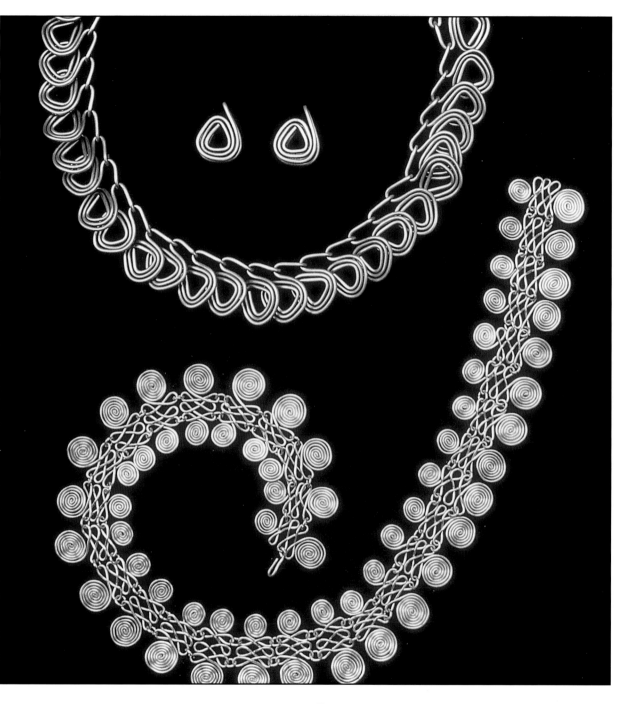

Top:

Chapter 10,
"Triangles."
Necklace and slip-on
earrings of copper
with an antiqued
finish.

Bottom:

Chapter Nine,
"Made On A Jig."
Necklace of copper
with a clear finish.

Top:
Chapter 11, "The Wave." Necklace of sterling silver.

Bottom:
Chapter 12, "B Bracelet." Bracelet and earrings of copper with an antiqued finish.

Top:

Chapter 13,
"An Expanding Belt."
Belt of low brass.

Bottom:

Chapter 14
"Daisy Chain."

Necklace and earrings
of copper and silver
plated wire with a
clear finish.

Chapter 15, "`Round and `Round."
Necklace and bracelet of brass with
a clear finish.

Figure 1

FIGURE EIGHTS

THIS BRACELET WAS FIRST MADE by twisting the wire into a figure eight with the round-nosed pliers. This meant moving the pliers along and making many small curves to produce a larger circle. We soon discovered how much easier and quicker it was to use a mandrel.

This is a large chain because we're using a thicker gauge wire. Chapter 26 shows how to make more delicate chains using variations in wire and mandrel size.

YOU WILL NEED:

36 5/8 inches (92.5 cm) of 14-gauge wire

A mandrel 3/8 inch (1 cm) in diameter, the approximate size of a #15 or #16 (US) knitting needle.

1. Wind 14-gauge wire around the mandrel. Stop winding when you have made 21 complete rounds of wire.

2. Remove the spring from the mandrel, cut it free from the spool or coil, and trim the ends.

3. Using the parallel pliers or flat-nosed pliers, bend six units of 3 1/2 rounds each away from the spring and cut them free. Each unit will look like Figure 2.

4. Open each unit at the point indicated in Figure 2, so that it looks like Figure 3.

5. Using the round-nosed pliers, pull the ends of each unit away from the circles, measuring each unit against Figure 4. File all the ends flat.

6. Loop each end of each unit, as shown in Figure 5. Then, using your fingers, bend each unit so that when the unit is lying flat as in Figure 5, the looped ends are a bit higher than the circles.

7. To make the hook and eye, cut one 3 1/8-inch (7.8 cm) length and

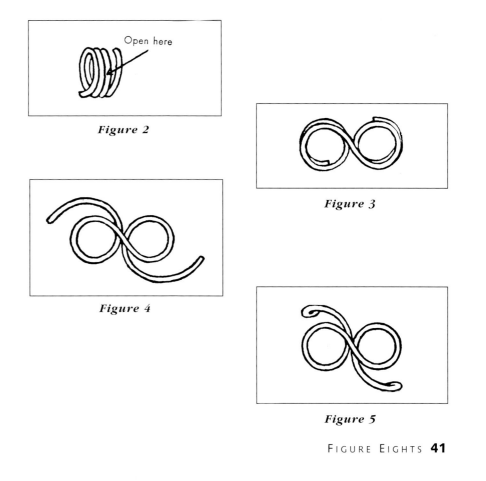

Figure 2

Figure 4

Figure 3

Figure 5

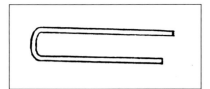

Figure 6

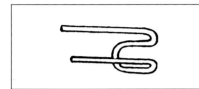

Figure 7

one 2-inch (5 cm) length of 14-gauge wire. File all the ends flat.

8. Using the parallel pliers or flat-nosed pliers, bend the 3 1/8-inch (7.8 cm) length to fit Figure 6, then to fit Figure 7. Next, use the round-nosed pliers to loop the ends as shown in Figure 8.

9. Bend the 2-inch (5 cm) length, and loop it as shown in Figure 8.

10. Using the parallel pliers or flat-nosed pliers and your fingers,

open the loops of each unit sideways, including the hook and eye.

11. Assemble the bracelet as shown in Figure 1, attaching the hook and eye as shown in Figure 8.

12. Bend each unit of the bracelet (except the hook and eye) at the center point, so that the whole bracelet will curve around the wrist of the wearer.

13. Apply a finish of your choice.

Figure 8

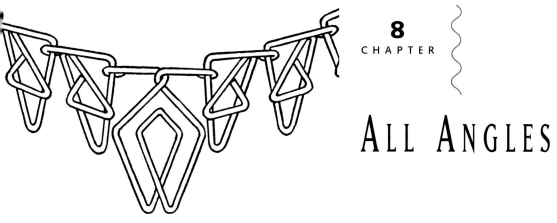

Figure 1

8

ALL ANGLES

A FRIEND MENTIONED SHE WAS intrigued with the look of extra-large paper clips and would like to see wire jewelry using the same design. On closer examination, we found that paper clips seemed too flat, so we made our links to overlap themselves in several places.

Once we started along these lines, more elaborate paper clips were inevitable. We use a small one here for the necklace and earrings, another one for a cuff link (Chapter 17), and the largest for—believe it or not—a paper clip! (Chapter 18)

YOU WILL NEED:

106 inches (2.6 m) of 14-gauge wire

1. To make the units for the right side of the necklace, cut 10 lengths of 14-gauge wire, each 4 3/4 (12 cm) inches long.

Straighten each length with your fingers. Then file all the ends flat.

2. Using the parallel or flat-nosed pliers, bend each length to fit against Figures 2, 3, 4, and 5. Remember

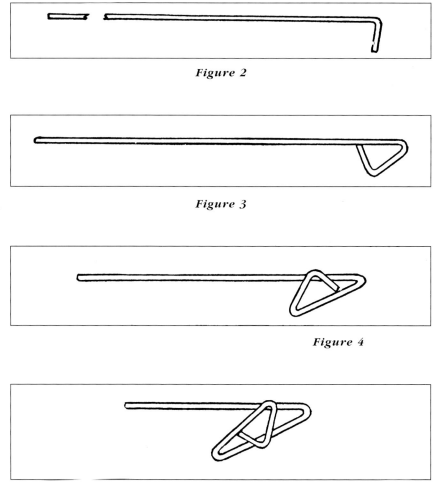

Figure 2

Figure 3

Figure 4

Figure 5

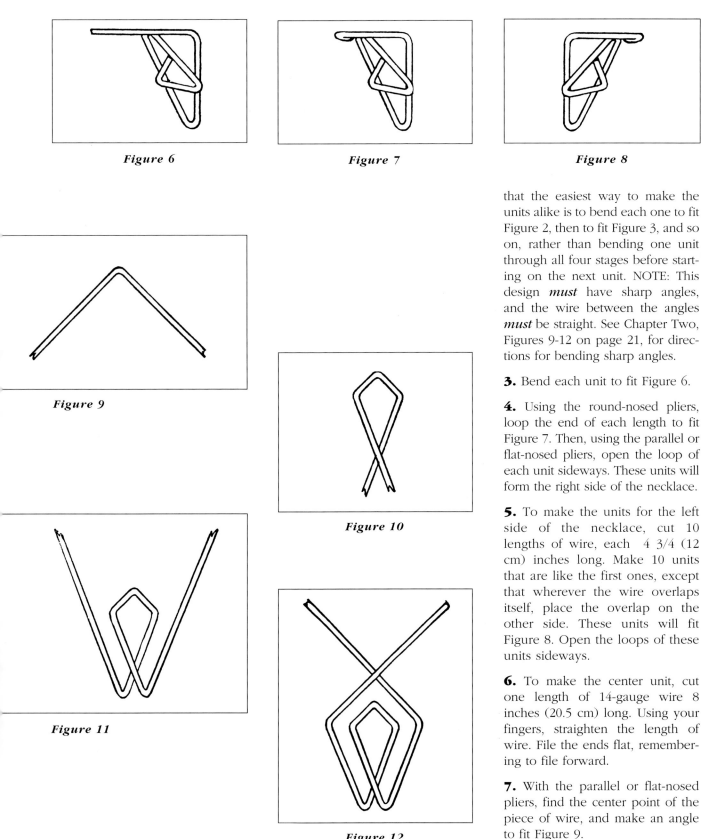

Figure 6

Figure 7

Figure 8

Figure 9

Figure 10

Figure 11

Figure 12

that the easiest way to make the units alike is to bend each one to fit Figure 2, then to fit Figure 3, and so on, rather than bending one unit through all four stages before starting on the next unit. NOTE: This design *must* have sharp angles, and the wire between the angles *must* be straight. See Chapter Two, Figures 9-12 on page 21, for directions for bending sharp angles.

3. Bend each unit to fit Figure 6.

4. Using the round-nosed pliers, loop the end of each length to fit Figure 7. Then, using the parallel or flat-nosed pliers, open the loop of each unit sideways. These units will form the right side of the necklace.

5. To make the units for the left side of the necklace, cut 10 lengths of wire, each 4 3/4 (12 cm) inches long. Make 10 units that are like the first ones, except that wherever the wire overlaps itself, place the overlap on the other side. These units will fit Figure 8. Open the loops of these units sideways.

6. To make the center unit, cut one length of 14-gauge wire 8 inches (20.5 cm) long. Using your fingers, straighten the length of wire. File the ends flat, remembering to file forward.

7. With the parallel or flat-nosed pliers, find the center point of the piece of wire, and make an angle to fit Figure 9.

8. Bend the unit to fit Figure 10. Next, bend the unit again to fit Figure 11. Then bend it once more to fit Figure 12.

9. Using the round-nosed pliers to start the twist evenly, twist each end around the other at the point where they now cross. Do not twist them just with your fingers. If you do this, you'll find that one end will use up more wire than the other, and the unit will not fit exactly on Figure 13 as it should.

10. Using the round-nosed pliers, loop each end as in Figure 14.

Open the loops of this unit.

11. For a hook, cut one length of 14-gauge wire 3 inches (7.5 cm) long. File one end round, the other flat. Loop the flat end. Bend the other end into a hook as shown in Figure 15.

12. Assemble the necklace as indicated in Figure 1, adding the hook as shown in Figure 15.

13. Apply a finish of your choice.

HOW TO MAKE SLIP-ON EARRINGS OF THIS DESIGN

YOU WILL NEED:

15 inches (38 cm) of 14-gauge wire

1. Cut two lengths of 14-gauge wire, each 7 1/2 (19 cm) inches long.

File all the ends flat.

2. Bend each length to fit Figure 17.

3. Using the round-nosed pliers, hold one of the units at the center point marked A.

4. Bend the ends of the unit toward each other to make an earring with two parallel sides, as shown in Figure 16. Bend the other unit in the same way.

5. Apply a finish of your choice.

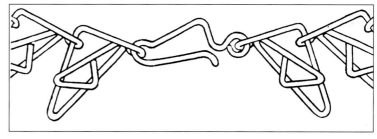

Figure 15

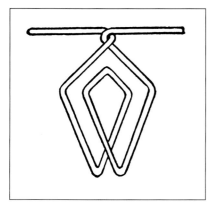

Figure 13

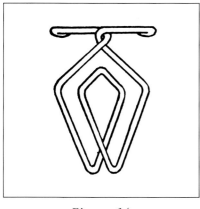

Figure 14

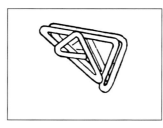

Figure 16

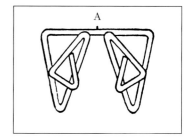

Figure 17

Figure 1

MADE ON A JIG

USING A JIG CAN BE FUN. IT'S A quick and easy way to make links for a bracelet or necklace that are all exactly alike. Some people find jigs fascinating and want to construct one for every design they tackle. If you're among them, you'll find it possible to make a jig for many of the units in the rest of the book. We only include detailed instructions for this one and another one in Chapter 27.

While we want you to know the possibilities of using a jig, we personally feel it's more fun to work in a freer style with fingers and pliers. Take note that the directions for a matching bracelet on page 47 call for making a different jig than the one you'll make for creating the necklace.

HOW TO MAKE A JIG FOR THE NECKLACE UNITS

YOU WILL NEED:

A small piece of wood hard enough to hold nails firmly. It should be at least 1 1/2 by 2 inches (4 cm x 5 cm), and 3/4 inch (2 cm) thick.

Six small nails or brads

A hammer

1. Trace this diagram (Figure 2) on a piece of paper, then glue it on the piece of wood.

2. Drive the six nails straight into the wood at the intersections of the lines in the diagram. Let them stick up about 1/4 inch (6 mm).

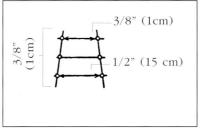

Figure 2

3. Using the wire cutters, cut the heads off the nails. File the ends of the nails smooth.

HOW TO MAKE A NECKLACE OF THIS DESIGN

YOU WILL NEED:

Approximately 405 inches (10 m) of 18-gauge wire

1 1/4 inches (3 cm) of 16-gauge wire

A mandrel 1/8 inch (3 mm) in diameter, the approximate size of a #3 (US) knitting needle

The jig you've just made

1. Cut 31 lengths of 18-gauge wire, each 12 inches (30.5 cm) long.

Mark each length of wire with a pencil line 3 (7.5 cm) inches from one end.

2. Place one of the lengths of wire on the jig so that the 3-inch (7.5 cm) portion is free, as indicated in Figure 3.

3. Wrap the wire tightly around the nails following the pattern in Figure 3. After the six loops have been made, there should be 5 inches (12.5 cm) of wire left straight. Remove the unit from the jig. Repeat these steps on the other lengths of wire.

4. Coil the ends of each unit to fit Figure 4.

5. To flatten and stiffen the units, first place several layers of newspaper on a sturdy table. Next, place a unit on top of the newspapers. Then, using a small mallet or the heel of a shoe, pound the unit. Remember, do not use a hammer with a metal head

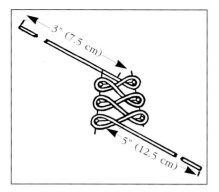

Figure 3

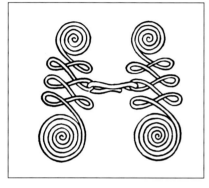

Figure 4

which will mark the wire even if the head is padded. Repeat these steps on the other units.

6. To make the jump rings, wind 18-gauge wire around the mandrel (#3 (US) knitting needle). Stop winding when you have made 60 complete rounds of wire. Remove this spring from the mandrel, cut it free from the spool or coil, and trim the ends.

7. Cut 60 jump rings. Open them sideways using the parallel or flat-nosed pliers and your fingers. File the ends of the jump rings flat.

8. To make the hook, cut one length of 16-gauge wire 1 1/4 inches (3 cm) long. File one end flat, the other round. Bend the wire with a loop on the flat end like the one shown in Figure 4.

9. Assemble the necklace as shown in Figure 1 at the head of

this chapter, with the hook attached to the center loops of the last unit, as shown in Figure 4.

10. Apply a finish of your choice.

HOW TO MAKE A MATCHING BRACELET

YOU WILL NEED:

130 inches (3.25 m) of 18-gauge wire

1 1/4 (3 cm) inches of 16-gauge wire

The jig shown in Figure 5

1. Make the jig shown in Figure 5, following Steps 1-3 in the directions for making the necklace jig.

NOTE: The guidelines on this jig are straight, unlike the lines on the jig for the necklace. The angled lines on the necklace jig give each unit a subtle curve that allows the assembled necklace to fit the neckline. This is unnecessary for fitting a bracelet to a wrist.

2. Cut 10 lengths of 18-gauge wire, each 12 inches (30.5 cm) long.

3. Mark each length with a pencil line 4 inches (10 cm) from one end.

4. In the same way you started the necklace units, place one of the lengths of wire on the jig so that the 4-inch (10 cm) end is free.

5. Wrap the wire tightly around the nails. You should have 4 inches (10 cm) of wire left straight after making six loops on the jig.

Repeat these steps on the other lengths of wire.

6. Coil both ends of each unit to fit Figure 6.

7. Flatten and stiffen the units the way you did the necklace units.

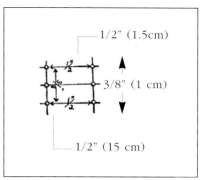

Figure 5

Figure 6

8. Wind 18-gauge wire around the mandrel (#3 (US) knitting needle) you used for the necklace. Stop winding when you have made 18 complete rounds of wire. Remove the spring from the mandrel, cut it free from the spool, and trim the ends.

9. Cut 18 jump rings. Then open them, using the parallel or flat-nosed pliers and your fingers. File all the ends of the jump rings flat.

10. For the hook, cut one length of 16-gauge wire 1 1/4 (3 cm) inches long. Bend the wire with a loop on the flat end as you did for Step 8 in the necklace directions.

11. Assemble the bracelet in the same way you did the necklace, including placement of the hook.

12. Apply a finish of your choice.

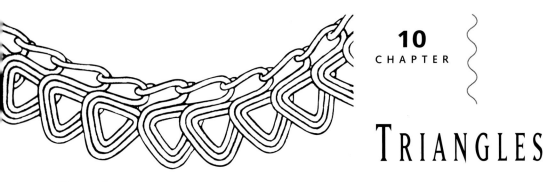

Figure 1

10
CHAPTER

TRIANGLES

THIS IS AN ADAPTATION OF THE Egyptian design in Chapter One that uses heavier wire and triangles instead of circles. You'll find this design is rather tricky to make because small differences will be more obvious than in most other designs. You may waste a few pieces of wire before you learn to make these units exactly alike. We recommend you make the necklace and earrings first. They're easier to make than the bracelet and will give you extra practice before tackling the more difficult piece.

2. Hold one end of one of the lengths of wire in the parallel or flat-nosed pliers, so that the edge of the pliers is 3/8 inches (1 cm) from the end. It's very important that this measurement be accurate.

3. Bend the wire into a right angle, pressing your thumb against the wire as close as possible to the point where it emerges from the pliers. Measure the bend against Figure 2. Repeat this operation on each of the lengths of wire, measuring each one against Figure 2.

NOTE: If you find that you are leaving tool marks on your work, cover the gripping surface of your pliers with adhesive tape.

4. Bend each length, using the parallel or flat-nosed pliers, to fit Figure 3.

5. Hold one of the units in the parallel pliers as in Figure 4.

Press with your left thumb, at the same time that you bend the wire with the pliers to produce a smaller angle.

6. Shift the pliers to the other right angle, and make it smaller in the same manner. Measure the unit against Figure 5. Repeat these steps on the other units, and measure each one against Figure 5.

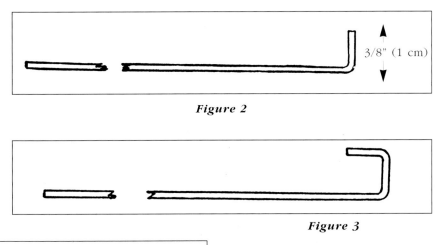

3/8" (1 cm)

Figure 2

Figure 3

___

YOU WILL NEED:

204 inches (5.1 m) of 14-gauge wire .

A mandrel 3/8 inch (1 cm) in diameter, the approximate size of a #15 or #16 (US) knitting needle

1. Cut 32 lengths of 14-gauge wire, each 6 1/4 inches (16 cm) long.

File all the ends flat.

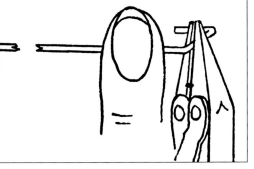

Figure 4

It is important that the angles are sharp and the sides of the triangle straight.

7. Hold one of the triangles in the pliers, as shown in Figure 6.

Bend the wire against the side of the triangle with your left thumb, as shown in Figure 7. Pull it away as in Figure 8, then bend it again sharply as in Figure 9. Bending the wire twice makes it lie close to the triangle. Repeat these steps on the other units.

8. Continue to bend the wire around the outside of the triangle. Shift the grip of the pliers when you are ready to make each sharp angle, then shift again when you have made the angle and are ready to press the wire against the side of the unit. Work on each unit in this way until there are three rounds on each side of the triangle, as in Figure 10. Repeat the process on the other units.

9. Bend the free end of one of the units back around the round-nosed pliers, as shown in Figure 11. Repeat this step on each of the units, and measure each against Figure 11.

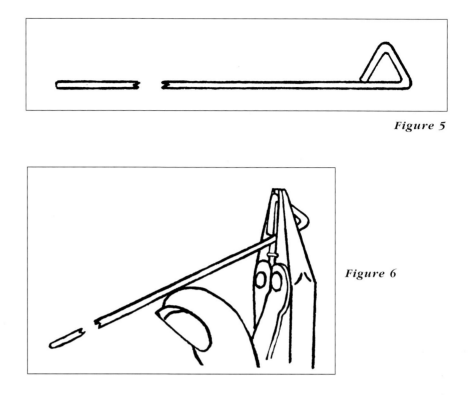

Figure 5

Figure 6

10. Using the wire cutters, cut off any end that is too long, and discard any unit with an end that is too short.

11. Using the round-nosed pliers, loop the end of each unit as shown in Figure 12. The loop should be round, not oval, and have an inside diameter of at least 1/8 inch (3.2 mm).

12. Push the loop of each unit a little closer to the triangle part of the unit, as in Figure 12.

13. Hold one of the units in your right hand, grasping it so that your fingers cover only the triangle, not the looped end. Push the looped end slightly away from you, so that the loop lies behind the triangle (see Figure 13). This operation is necessary to make the units overlap after they're assembled. Repeat this operation on each unit. Then open the loop of each unit sideways.

14. For the hook, cut one 2 1/2-inch (6.5 cm) length of 14-gauge wire. File one end round, the other flat. Make a hook on the round end, a loop on the flat end. Open the loop sideways.

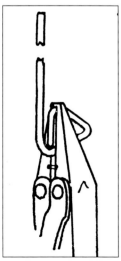

Figure 7

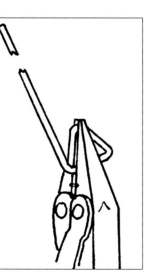

Figure 8

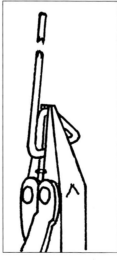

Figure 9

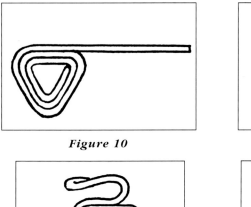

Figure 10

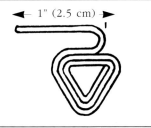

Figure 11

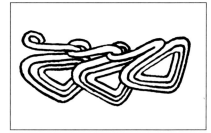

Figure 14

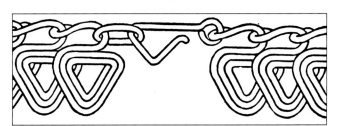

Figure 12

Figure 13

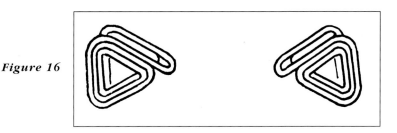

Figure 15

2. Bend each end of each length of wire into a triangle just like the first triangle of the necklace units. Measure against Figures 2, 3, and 5 on pages 48-49.

3. Bend the wire around the outside of each of the triangles, until you have two units that fit against Figure 17.

4. Using the round-nosed pliers, hold the center point of one of the units as shown in Figure 18.

5. Bend the triangles toward each other to form an earring like the ones in Figure 16. Be sure to keep the two sides parallel. Bend the other unit in the same way.

6. Apply a finish of your choice.

15. Cut a jump ring from the spring you made for "A Simple Chain." (If you do not have a spring on hand, see page 22.) Open the jump ring sideways. File the ends of the jump ring flat.

16. Assemble the necklace as shown in Figures 14 and 15.

17. Apply a finish of your choice.

HOW TO MAKE MATCHING EARRINGS

YOU WILL NEED:

21 inches (53.5 cm) of 14-gauge wire

1. Cut two lengths of 14-gauge wire, each 10 1/2 inches (26.5 cm) long. File all the ends flat.

HOW TO MAKE A TRIANGLE BRACELET

YOU WILL NEED:

146 1/2 inches (3.7 m) of 14-gauge wire.

1. Cut 11 lengths of 14-gauge wire, each 12 inches (30.5 cm) long.

File all ends flat.

2. Bend each end of each length of wire into a triangle just like the first triangle of the necklace units. Measure against Figures 2, 3, and 5 on pages 48-49.

3. Continue bending the wire around the outside of the triangles. Repeat this step until you have 11 units that fit against Figure 20.

Figure 16

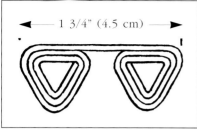

1 3/4" (4.5 cm)

Figure 17

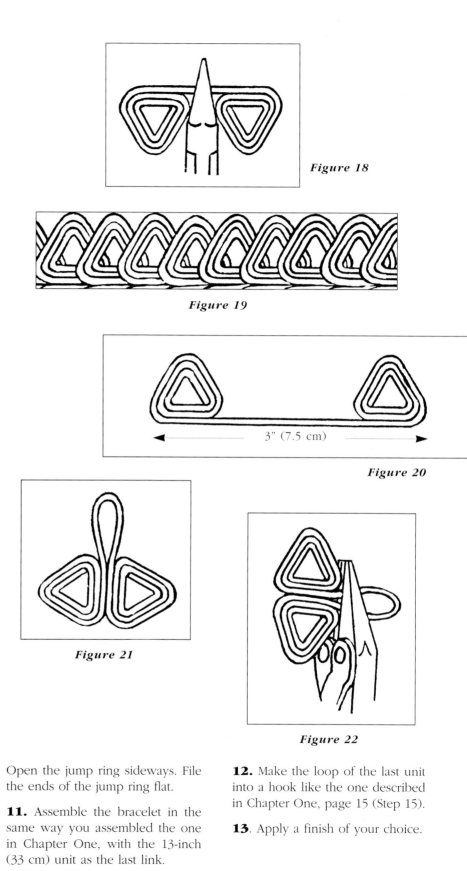

Figure 18

Figure 19

3" (7.5 cm)

Figure 20

Figure 21

Figure 22

4. Using the round-nosed pliers, hold the center point of one of the units. Position the pliers at a right angle to the unit. Do not position them in the same plane as they were when you bent the earring units.

5. Bend the unit to fit Figure 21. Repeat this operation on each of the units, and measure each one against Figure 21.

6. Hold one of the units as shown in Figure 22. Using your fingers, bend the triangles down at a right angle to the loop.

7. For the hook end, cut one length of 14-gauge wire 13 inches (33 cm) long. File the ends flat.

8. Bend the length of wire the same way you did with the other units. When you reach the stage shown in Figure 20, this unit will be 4 inches (10 cm) long instead of 3 inches (7.5 cm). After the next operation, it will be 1 7/8 inches (4.7 cm) long and have a long loop like the unit you made for a hook in Chapter One, page 15, (Figure 23).

9. Hold this unit in the parallel pliers as shown in Figure 22, with the edge of the pliers just above the triangles, and the longer loop extending to the right. Bend the triangles down at a right angle to the loop, as you bent the other units.

10. Cut a jump ring from the spring you made for Chapter Three. (If you do not have a spring left, see page 22 for instructions.)

Open the jump ring sideways. File the ends of the jump ring flat.

11. Assemble the bracelet in the same way you assembled the one in Chapter One, with the 13-inch (33 cm) unit as the last link.

12. Make the loop of the last unit into a hook like the one described in Chapter One, page 15 (Step 15).

13. Apply a finish of your choice.

Figure 1

11
CHAPTER

THE WAVE

EVEN THOUGH ITS LINKS LOOK large, "The Wave" is lightweight and easy to wear. You may want to try making it in sterling silver since it requires fewer inches of wire than other designs. However, we recommend you make it in copper or brass first before working with the higher-priced silver.

120 inches (3 m) of 14-gauge wire

1. Cut 11 lengths of 14-gauge wire, each 10 1/2 inches (26.5 cm) long. File all the ends flat.

2. Grasp one of the lengths at a point 6 inches (15 cm) from one end, using the base of the round-nosed pliers. Curve the wire as shown in Figure 2.

3. Continue to hold the wire at the same point. Bend the end that measures 6 inches (15 cm) (B in Figure 2) into a reverse curve larger than the first loop. Repeat these steps on the other units, measuring each one against Figure 3 as you complete it.

4. Using your fingers, bend the other end (marked A) of each unit around the outside of B, measuring each one against Figure 4.

5. Again using your fingers, bend end B of each unit around the outside of A, measuring each one against Figure 5.

6. Bend A across the top of each unit, and measure the units against Figure 6. Cut off any ends that are too long.

7. Loop the ends of each unit as shown in Figure 7. Using the parallel or flat-nosed pliers, open the smaller loop at end B on each unit.

8. For the hook, cut a 3-inch (7.5 cm) length of 14-gauge wire. File one end flat, the other round. Make a hook on the rounded end,

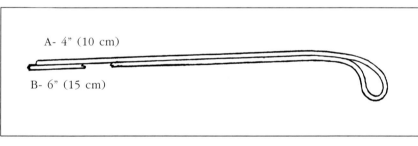

A- 4" (10 cm)

B- 6" (15 cm)

Figure 2

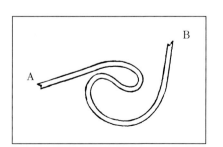

A

B

Figure 3

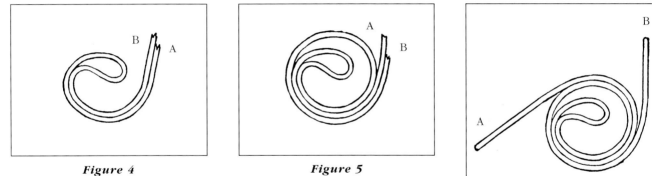

Figure 4

Figure 5

Figure 6

like the one shown in Chapter Six, Figure 8, page 32.

9. Cut a jump ring from the spring you made for Chapter Three (or see page 22, if you do not have a spring). Open the jump ring sideways, using the parallel or flat-nosed pliers and your fingers.

File the ends of the jump ring flat.

10. Assemble the necklace by hooking the opened loop of each unit through the closed loop of the next unit and closing it with the parallel or flat-nosed pliers. In the same way, attach the jump ring to one end of the necklace and the hook to the other.

11. Apply a finish of your choice.

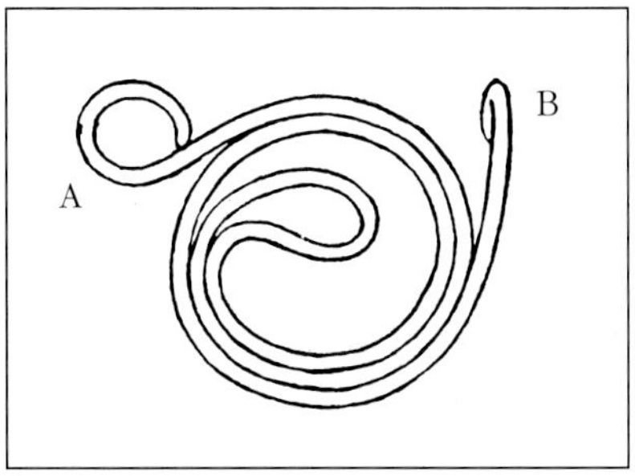

Figure 7

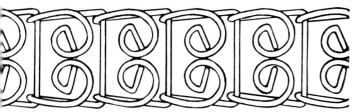

Figure 1

"B" Bracelet and Belt

DOES THIS DESIGN SUGGEST A LETTER B to you? It got its name because several people saw the same thing. This design works for a bracelet and belt but not for a necklace because its individual links will not form the graceful curve that a series of links must make to shape a necklace.

You can use an old buckle of your own for the belt—a plain, rectangular or square one works best. Or, you can create the spiral buckle we suggest on page 56 made from heavy wire. We specify 8-gauge wire for this buckle, the only place in this book where you'll use such a heavy gauge. You

might have some luck finding this gauge in brass or copper at a hardware store.

Otherwise, you may need to order it from a jewelry supply catalog.

HOW TO MAKE THE BRACELET

YOU WILL NEED:

69 inches (1.7 m) of 14-gauge wire

1. Cut 10 lengths of 14-gauge wire, each 6 1/2 inches (16.5 cm) long. File all the ends round.

2. Bend each length to fit Figure 2, holding the end in the parallel or flat-nosed pliers to make the first sharp angle. Then bend the curve with your fingers. Be sure this part of the design fits Figure 2 exactly. If it's not right, the whole unit will be wrong.

3. Hold one of the units in the parallel or flat-nosed pliers so that the edge of the pliers is at Point A (see Figure 2). Bend the wire back against the top of the pliers, and measure it against Figure 3. Flatten the bend with your fingers.

4. Hold the same unit in the parallel or flat-nosed pliers so that the edge of the pliers is at Point B (Figure 2), and bend the wire in the same manner, so that the unit fits Figure 3. Repeat these steps on the other units.

5. Using the parallel or flat-nosed pliers, bend each unit to fit Figure 4. In each case the edge of the pliers will be at Point C, then at Point D when you bend the wire (Figure 3).

6. For the hook, cut one length of 14-gauge wire 4 inches (10 cm)

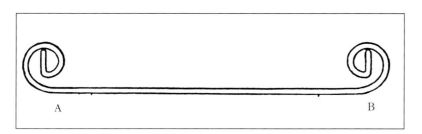

Figure 2

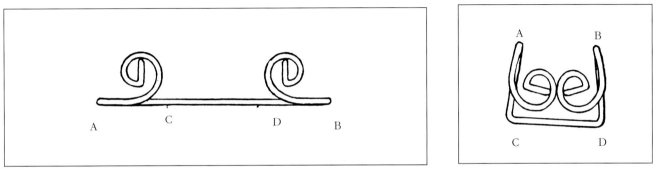

Figure 3

Figure 4

long. File the ends flat. Loop both ends of this length.

Bend it to fit the drawing of the hook shown in Figure 5.

7. Assemble the bracelet, with the hook on one end as shown in Figure 5. To hook one unit onto the next, slip the two coiled ends of one unit through the space between the coils and the bar of the next unit. Then press the coiled ends of the first unit down flat so that the links will not come apart.

8. Apply a finish of your choice.

Figure 5

HOW TO MAKE A BELT OF THIS DESIGN

YOU WILL NEED:

213 inches (5.3 m) of 14-gauge wire for a belt that will fit a 26- to 27-inch (66 cm to 68.5 cm) waist.

A buckle from your collection, or 16 inches (40.5 cm) of 8-gauge wire

NOTE: Each unit of the belt adds about 3/4 inch (2 cm) to the length of the belt. If you know the waist measurement, you can count on fewer or more links as needed. These measurements are figured with the 8-gauge buckle, which expands from 1 1/2 inches (4 cm) to 3 inches (7.5 cm). Without the buckle or the hook, 32 links will make the belt approximately 24 inches (61 cm) long.

1. Cut 32 lengths of 14-gauge wire, each 6 1/2 inches (16.5 cm) long.

2. Make and assemble 32 links just like the ones you made for the bracelet.

3. Cut one length of 14-gauge wire 5 inches (12.5 cm) long. File the ends flat.

4. Make a unit to hold the buckle, like the one shown in Figure 6, and in a side view in Figure 7.

5. Cut one 16-inch length of 8-gauge wire to make the buckle.

File the ends round.

6. Bend this length to fit the spiral buckle shown in Figure 6, Use the parallel or flat-nosed pliers to make the first sharp angle, then use your fingers to shape the rest of the spiral.

NOTE: The wearer can wind the spiral around in either direction (see Figure 6), bringing the ends of the belt closer or farther apart.

7. Attach the unit you made in Step 4 to hold the spiral as shown in Figure 6.

8. Apply a finish of your choice.

Figure 6

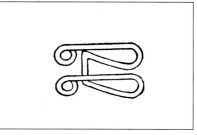

Figure 7

HOW TO MAKE EARRINGS TO GO WITH THE BRACELET

YOU WILL NEED:

12 inches (30.5 cm) of 14-gauge wire.

1. Cut two lengths of 14-gauge wire, each 6 inches (15 cm) long.

File all the ends round.

2. Bend each length, using the parallel or flat-nosed pliers to make the first sharp angle. Then use your fingers to make the rest of the coils. Measure each one to fit Figure 9.

3. Using the round-nosed pliers, hold one of the units at its center point. Bend it to make an earring like the one shown in Figure 8. Remember, to fit properly, these slip-on earrings must have parallel sides (see Chapter Five, page 30).

4. Apply a finish of your choice.

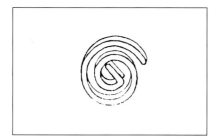

Figure 8

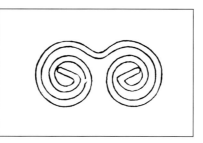

Figure 9

GALLERY

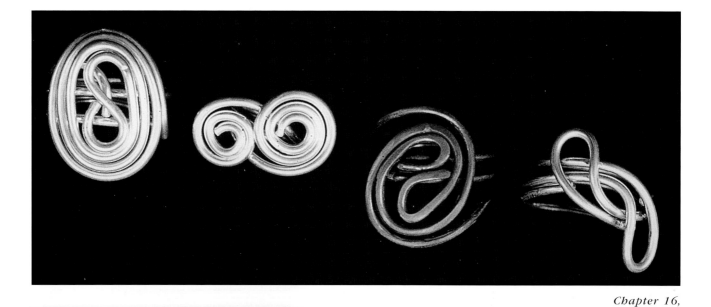

Chapter 16,
"Four Rings,"
of sterling silver.

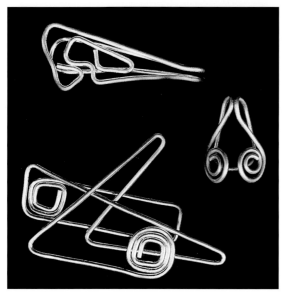

Chapter 18, "Clips."
Top: *Tie clip of sterling silver.*
Bottom: *Clips of brass and copper*

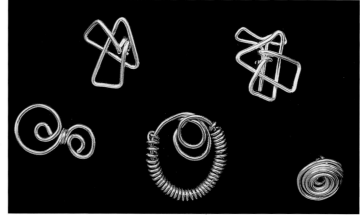

Chapter 17, "Buttons and Cuff Links."
Top: *Cuff links of sterling silver.*
Bottom: *Buttons of copper and*
low brass.

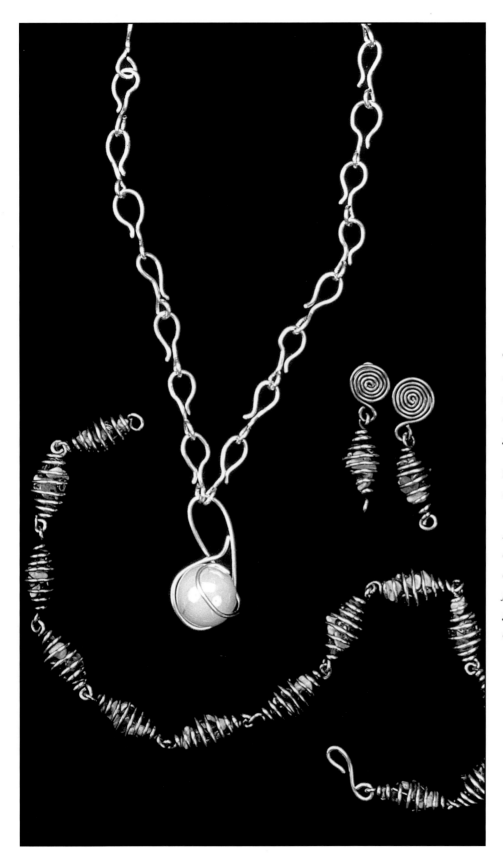

Top:

*Chapter 20, "Chain
with Pendant,"
of sterling silver with
glass marble.*

Bottom:

*Chapter 19,
"Bird Cages."
Necklace and
earrings of
copper with antiqued
finish. Multicolored
gemstones fill the
cages.*

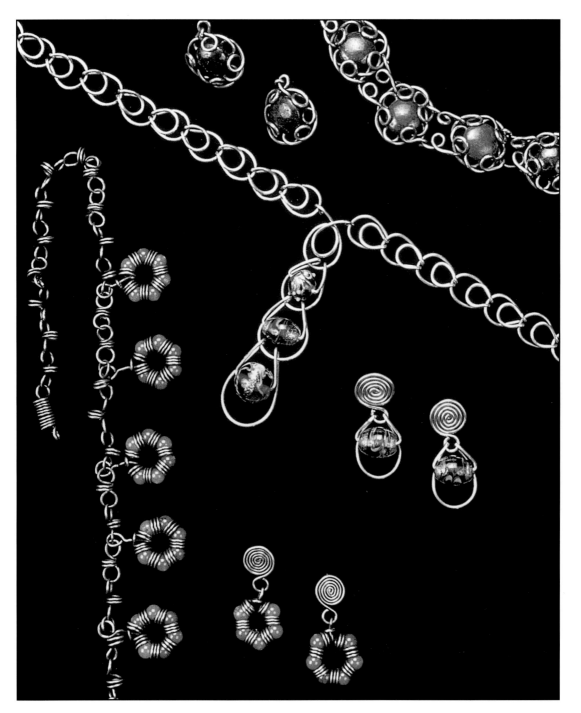

Clockwise:
Chapter 21,
"Loop the Loop."
Bracelet and
earrings of copper
with antiqued
finish;

Chapter 23,
"Triple Pendant."
Necklace and
earrings of brass
with glass beads and
clear finish;

Chapter 22,
"Colorful Dangles."
Necklace and ear-
rings of copper with
antiqued finish.

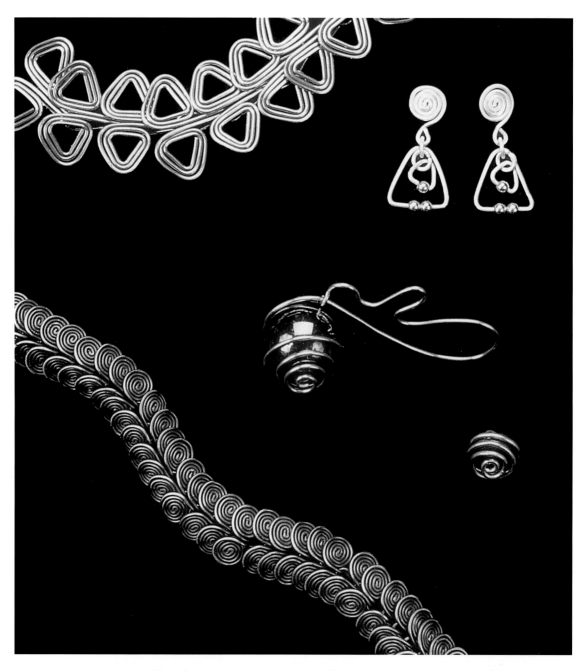

Clockwise:
Chapter 25,
"Variations of
the Egyptian."
Bracelet "A" of
copper with
clear finish;

Chapter 24,
"A Few Extras."
Earrings of sterling
silver with gold
beads. Key chain
of copper with
multicolored marble.
Button of brass
with clear finish;

Chapter 25,
"Variations of the
Egyptian."
Bracelet "B" of
annealed wire.

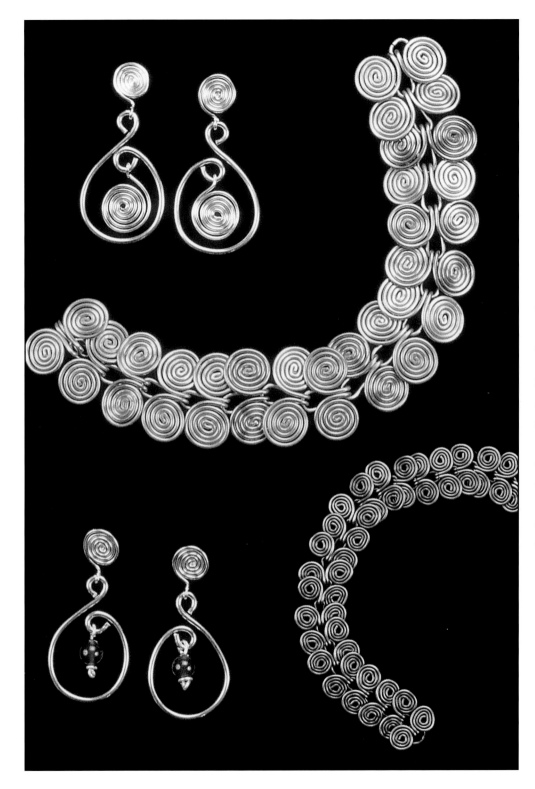

Chapter 25,
"Variations on the
Egyptian."

Clockwise:
Earrings of sterling sil-
ver; bracelet "D"
of copper, high brass,
and low brass with
clear finish; bracelet
"C" of copper with
antiqued finish; ear-
rings in sterling silver.

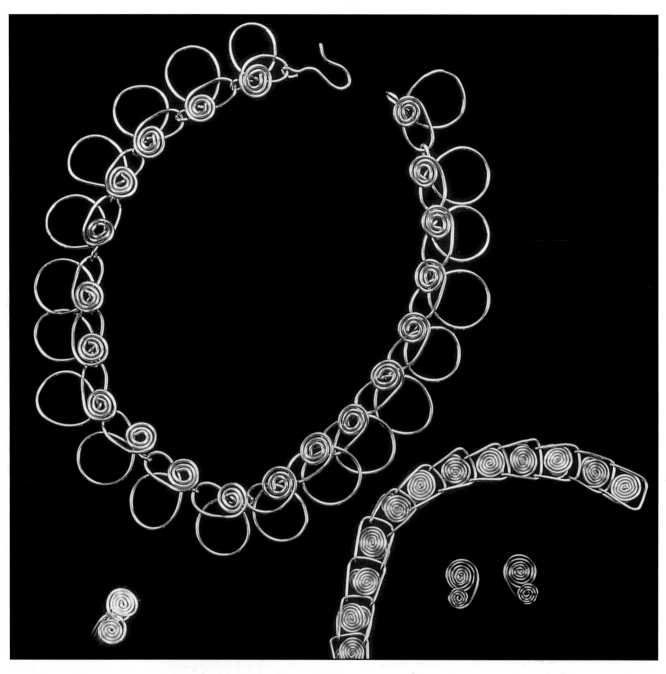

Chapter 25,
"Variations on the
Egyptian."

Clockwise:
Necklace using coils
of brass with clear
finish; bracelet using
Egyptian coils of
copper with a
clear finish;

coil earrings of teal
niobium; ring of
sterling silver.

*Chapter 26,
"Chains."*

Left to right:
*Chain "C" of
sterling silver;
chain "B" of sterling
silver and niobium;
chain "A" of brass
with clear finish;
chain "D" of
sterling silver.*

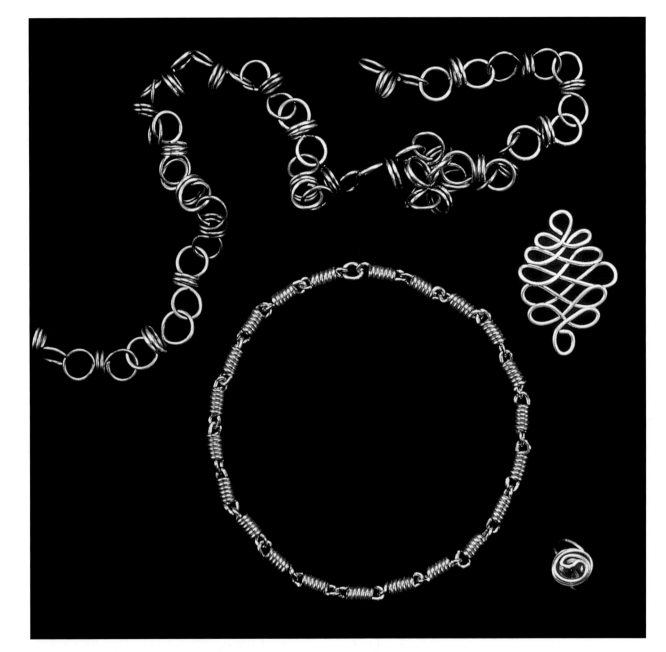

Counter clockwise:

Chapter 26, "Chains," chain "F" of silver, copper and brass with antique finish; choker of copper;

Chapter 27, "Adaptations," ring of sterling silver; central necklace unit of sterling silver.

Figure 1

13
CHAPTER

AN EXPANDING BELT

THE ELASTIC PROPERTY OF THIS belt combines high-fashion appeal with comfort. You can use the fastening described in the directions or use your own buckle.

If you have trouble figuring out how to attach a ready-made buckle, look through the book for suggestions. At this point, you should be able to devise something that will enable you to attach a buckle to the ends of the belt links.

If your buckle won't work with any ideas in the other projects, try creating a connecting length of your own by sketching your designs on paper. Figure out where you must attach the wire to the buckle and to the ends of the belt link. Connect these points with a line that represents the wire and you'll begin to see potential solutions.

YOU WILL NEED:

166 1/4 inches (4.2 m) of 14-gauge wire

1. Cut 25 lengths of 14-gauge wire, each 6 1/4 inches (16 cm) long. File all the ends round.

NOTE: You can estimate that one unit will measure about 1 inch

(2.5 cm) since we've found that 25 units (with the buckle, which adds 1 1/2 inches (4 cm) will make a belt 26 1/2 inches (64.5 cm) long. Add or subtract units for the desired measurement. Make sure, however, that the finished belt has an uneven number of links, or the buckle will have to be redesigned.

2. Curve each length at the center to fit Figure 2.

3. Using the round-nosed pliers and then your fingers, loop each unit to fit Figure 3.

4. Loop the other end of each unit so that it fits figure 4. As you bend

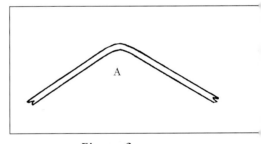

Figure 2

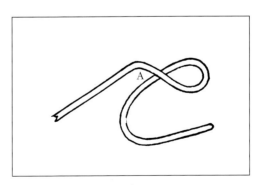

Figure 3

Figure 4

Figure 5

the wire back with your fingers to make the curve marked A in Figure 4, be sure that you bring it under the other end, then over it, as the figure indicates.

5. Loop each end of each unit, as shown in Figure 5. Open all the end loops sideways.

6. To make the two buckle units, cut one 4-inch (10 cm) length and one 6-inch (15 cm) length of 14-gauge wire. File all the ends flat.

7. Using the round-nosed pliers, loop one end of each length to make a small loop like the ones on the ends of the other links.

8. Using your fingers and then the round-nosed pliers, bend the 4-inch (10 cm) length to fit the unit marked A in Figure 6. Next, again using your fingers and then the round-nosed pliers, bend the 6-inch (15 cm) length to fit the unit marked B in Figure 6. Fit B and A together as in Figure 6 so that when they are hooked the belt will lie straight.

9. Assemble the belt with alternating units upside down, as shown in Figure 1. Attach the hook-and-eye fastening you have just made to the ends as shown in Figure 6.

10. Apply a finish of your choice.

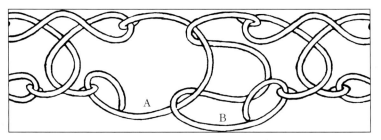

Figure 6

Figure 1

14
CHAPTER

DAISY CHAIN

DON'T LET THE LACY APPEARANCE of this necklace deceive you. It's not as hard as you might think. Once you get started you'll be surprised at how easy it is to make, not unlike stringing a fresh daisy chain on a summer afternoon.

YOU WILL NEED:

175 inches (4.3 m) of 18-gauge wire

8 inches (20.5 cm) of 16-gauge wire

Two mandrels the same size shown in Figure 2, the approximate size of #3 (US) knitting needles

A mandrel 5/16 inch (8 mm) in diameter, the approximate size of a #13 (US) knitting needle

NOTE: There are several different ways to hold the mandrels for wrapping the wire as shown in Figure 2:

A. Hold the two #3 (US) needles (or their equivalent) in your left

hand so that they are parallel and about 1/4 inch (6 mm) apart.

B. Place the knitting needles parallel to each other, 1/4 inch (6 mm) apart. Using masking tape as a separator, tape the two knitting needles at their blunt end so they remain 1/4 inch (6 mm) apart and parallel. Place the knitting needles on a table with most of their length overhanging the edge. Tape them to the table in this position. This anchors the needles, freeing both your hands while you wrap.

C. Place the knitting needle in a vise 1/4 inch (6 mm) apart and parallel.

1. Wind the 18-gauge wire in and out around the two needles with a figure-eight motion, keeping the loops as close together as possible (Figure 2). Stop winding when you've made 120 figure eights. (If your mandrels are not long enough, make eight units of 15 figure eights each.)

2. Cut the wire between the figure eights so that you have eight units of 15 figure eights.

3. Using your fingers, curve each unit into a fan shape so that it looks like Figure 3. File the ends of each unit flat.

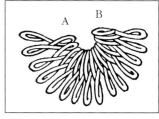

Figure 2

Figure 3

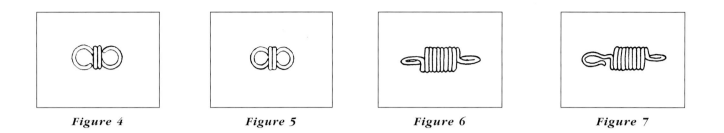

| Figure 4 | Figure 5 | Figure 6 | Figure 7 |

4. Using the round-nosed pliers, close the end loops of each unit so that it looks like Figure 3, with the ends at Points A and B tight against the unit as shown.

5. Make eight jump rings by winding 16-gauge wire around a #13 (US) knitting needle (or its equivalent). Open the jump rings sideways.

File all the ends flat.

6. Insert each jump ring through the inner loops of one of the 18-gauge units. Close each jump ring, turning it so that the joint is hidden inside the 18-gauge unit (see Figure 1). If you find that these jump rings fit too tight, make them slightly larger by using a slightly larger mandrel.

7. Wind 18-gauge wire around one #3 (US) knitting needle (or its equivalent) to make 98 complete rounds. Cut 10 jump rings from one end of this spring. Open the jump rings sideways, and file them flat.

8. To make the chain, cut 16 units of four rounds each from the remainder of the spring. To make the clasp, cut two units of 12 rounds each from the spring.

9. Using the parallel or flat-nosed pliers, bend one complete round on each end of each four-round unit away from the center rounds (see Figure 4).

10. Push the ends of each unit down into the center rounds and against the inside (Figure 5). Using the parallel or flat-nosed pliers, open one end round of each of these units sideways.

11. Assemble two chains of eight units each, inserting the open loop of each unit through the closed loop of the next and then closing it.

12. Loop both ends of one of the 12-round units, and one end of the other 12-round unit. The first will make the eye for the second, which will be the hook.

13. Using the round-nosed pliers, bend the other end of the second 12-round unit to make a hook like the one shown in Figure 7.

Attach the hook to the end of one chain, the eye to the end of the other chain.

14. Assemble the fan-shaped 18-gauge units as shown in Figure 1, using jump rings to join them at the points indicated. Two of the fan-shaped units are not shown in the figure. Attach them to the units shown with jump rings. Figure 8 shows how these end units look, and how the eight-unit chain is attached at either end of the center part of the necklace.

15. Apply a finish of your choice.

NOTE: You can make earrings for pierced ears to match this necklace in three steps.

1. Make two 18-gauge units as shown in Figure 3.

2. Make two jump rings and attach them to the 18-gauge units following Steps 5 and 6.

3. Attach a commercial French wire to the jump rings.

Figure 8

Figure 1

'ROUND AND 'ROUND

IN THIS DESIGN, WE'VE DOUBLED the wire to make a heavier looking and more substantial bracelet than would be otherwise possible with 16-gauge wire. On page 70 you will find a necklace that is similar in design but does not match the bracelet exactly. When you pair them, you'll have a set that adds the interest of harmonizing patterns.

YOU WILL NEED:

---

66 1/2 inches (1.6 m) of 16-gauge wire

1. Cut 10 lengths of 16-gauge wire, each 6 1/2 inches (16.5 cm) long.File all ends flat.

2. Using the round-nosed pliers, hold one of the lengths at a point 3 inches (7.5 cm) from one end. Bend the length to fit Figure 2. Repeat this step on all of the lengths.

3. Using the round-nosed pliers, hold one of the units at the point marked A in Figure 2. Bend the shorter end around to make the curve marked B in Figure 3. Curve the shorter end to fit Figure 3.

Repeat these steps on the other units.

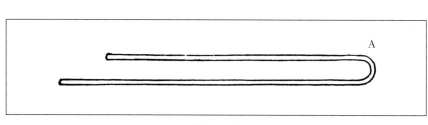

Figure 2

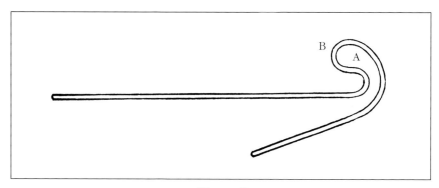

Figure 3

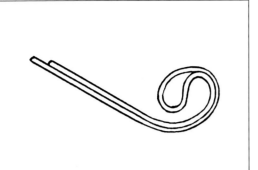

Figure 4

Figure 5

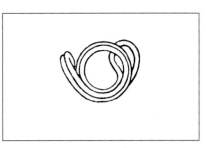

Figure 6

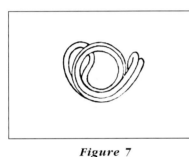

Figure 7

Figure 8

Put aside five of the units, and perform the next steps on the other five.

4. Curve the long end around and slightly under the short end to fit Figure 4. Using your fingers, curve both ends to fit Figure 5. The shorter end of the wire should be kept slightly overlapping the longer end so that the inner circle is always smaller than, and partly on top of, the outer circle.

5. Loop both ends of each unit in the same direction so that each of the five units looks like Figure 6.

6. Bend the other five lengths of wire in the same manner, except that the double circles will be on the other side of the first curve. These units will look like Figure 7 when they are finished. Check

them against that figure as you complete each step on each unit.

7. Using the parallel or flat-nosed pliers, open the loops on the ends of all ten units. On each unit, open one of the loops to the left and one to the right.

8. For the hook, cut one length of 16-gauge wire 1 1/2 inches (4 cm) long. File one end flat, the other round. Loop the flat end. Bend the rounded end into a hook, as in Figure 8. Open the loop.

9. Assemble the bracelet with alternating units upside down, as is indicated in Figure 1, and attach the hook as shown in Figure 8.

10. Apply a finish of your choice.

NECKLACE-A COMPANION PIECE

This necklace provides a three-dimensional look. It's a good companion piece for the bracelet you just made.

YOU WILL NEED:

168 1/2 inches (4.2 m) of 14-gauge wire

1. Cut 15 lengths of 14-gauge wire, each 11 inches (28 cm) long.

File all the ends flat.

2. Using the round-nosed pliers, hold the lengths at a point 6 inches (15 cm) from one end. Bend the wire to make a curve that fits Figure 10.

Figure 9

3. Continue to hold the unit in the round-nosed pliers as shown in Figure 11. Bend both ends of the wire at the same time to fit Figure 12. The end marked A should be tight against and on top of the end marked B. Repeat these steps on the other lengths, measuring each against Figure 12.

4. Using the parallel or flat-nosed pliers, hold one of the units as in Figure 13. Using your fingers, bend both ends together with A still overlapping B, as shown in Figure 14. Do not let the wire make any sharp bends, try to keep the curve a gradual, smooth one. As the ends approach the loop, guide them up through it.

5. Pull both ends up through the loop, and bend them back as shown in Figure 15, If the ends are uneven in length, cut them to fit Figure 15. Repeat these steps on the other units, and measure each one against Figure 15.

6. Using the round-nosed pliers, loop both ends of each unit so that each unit looks like Figure 16 from the back.

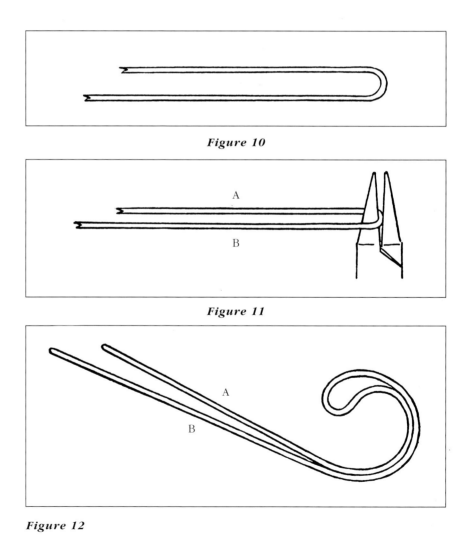

Figure 10

Figure 11

Figure 12

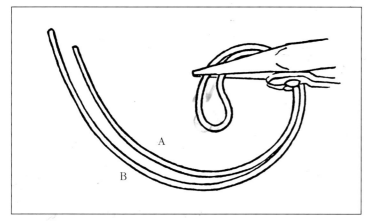

Figure 13

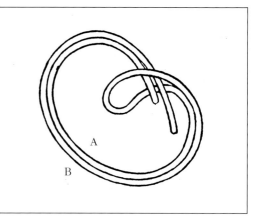

Figure 14

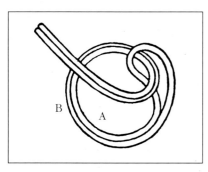

Figure 15

Figure 16

7. For the hook, cut one 2-inch (5 cm) length of 14-gauge wire to make the hook. File one end flat, the other round. Loop the flat end. Make a hook on the other end, like the one shown in Chapter Three on page 23 (Step 12). Open the loop sideways.

8. Cut a jump ring from the spring you made for Chapter Three (or see page 22 if you do not have a spring). Open the jump ring sideways. File the ends of the jump ring flat.

9. Assemble the necklace as shown in Figure 1 at the head of this chapter, with the hook on the end that has two loops on it, and the jump ring on the other end.

10. Apply a finish of your choice.

A   B   C   D

Figure 1

FOUR RINGS

As you continue to work with wire, you'll find there are many other pieces of jewelry that you can make aside from necklaces, bracelets, and earrings. In the next few chapters we present some suggestions for other accessories which should give you an idea of the possibilities.

Having worked through the previous projects, you should feel confident enough to use the principles we've presented to create pieces that fill your individual interests and needs. Feel free to vary the designs wherever you see that another twist would do just as well. In Chapters 25-27 we present many variations on techniques you've already learned. You'll probably find Chapter 28 on designing more useful if you want to try making rings, lapel pins, buttons, cuff links, tie clasps, paper clips, and so on for your own special use.

NOTE: In specifying the length of wire to be cut for a ring, we can only approximate an average size. You will need to measure the finger to be fitted and add or subtract the necessary length. Practice with copper or brass wire if you are not sure.

TO MAKE THE RING LETTERED A IN FIGURE 1

YOU WILL NEED:

Approximately 8 1/2 inches (21.5 cm) of 14-gauge wire

1. Cut one 8 1/2-inch (21.5 cm) length of 14-gauge wire. File the ends round.

2. Loop each end of the wire, then coil it to fit Figure 2.

3. Using your fingers, bend the wire to form the part of the ring that goes around the finger. Start at one end and make a circle at a right angle to the coil. Continue the circle, making two complete rounds, ending with the coils on the top, as in Figure 1.

4. Place the ring on your finger and press the coils down at the outer edges so that they follow the contour of the finger instead of being in a flat plane.

5. Apply a finish of your choice.

TO MAKE THE RING LETTERED B IN FIGURE 1

YOU WILL NEED:

Approximately 14 inches (35.5 cm) of 14-gauge wire.

1. Cut a 14-inch (35.5 cm) length of 14-gauge wire. File the ends round.

2. Using the round-nosed pliers, bend one end of the wire to fit Figure 3.

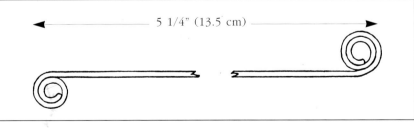

5 1/4" (13.5 cm)

Figure 2

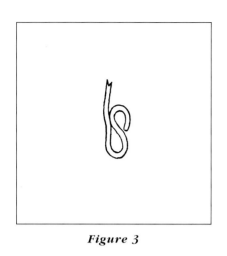

Figure 3

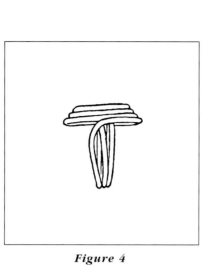

Figure 4

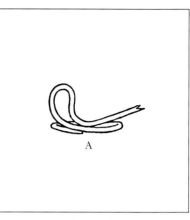

Figure 5

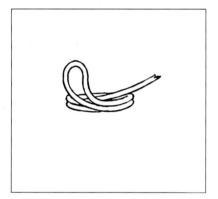

Figure 6

Figure 7

3. Using your fingers to bend the wire around the outside of the S-shape, make three complete rounds (see Figure 1). As you bend, push each round a little under the edge of the one inside it. Doing this ensures that this part of the ring, which will lie on top of the finger, will have a raised center. Figure 4 shows how it should look from the side.

4. To start the part of the ring that goes around the finger, bend the wire at a right angle to the part you just made. Make three rounds, which should form circles, the tops of which come up under the center of the design and support it.

5. Using the round-nosed pliers, tuck the end of the wire up against the inside of the design on the top of the ring. This will prevent the wearer from getting scratched.

6. Apply a finish of your choice.

NOTE: You may be able to adapt the S-shape to make other initials for personalized initial rings.

TO MAKE THE RING LETTERED C IN FIGURE 1

YOU WILL NEED:

Approximately 10 inches (25.5 cm) of 14-gauge wire.

1. Cut a 10-inch (25.5 cm) length of 14-gauge wire. File the ends round.

2. Bend one end of the wire around your finger. The point marked A in Figure 5 shows the first circle. Then loop the wire as shown in Figure 5.

3. Bend the wire around your finger again to make another circle next to the first as in Figure 6.

4. Loop the wire again as shown in Figure 7.

5. Once more, bend the wire around your finger.

6. Apply a finish of your choice.

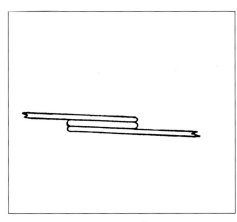

Figure 8

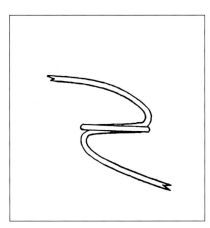

Figure 9

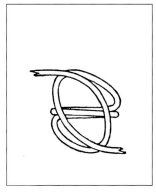

Figure 10

TO MAKE THE RING LETTERED D IN FIGURE 1

YOU WILL NEED:

Approximately 10 inches (25.5 cm) of 14-gauge wire.

1. Cut a 10-inch (25.5 cm) length of 14-gauge wire. File the ends round.

2. Starting in the center of the wire, bend the wire around your finger to make a double circle. After you do this, both ends should be the same length, and the center of the wire will look like Figure 8.

3. Using your fingers, pull the ends of the wire apart as shown in Figure 9. Then continue to use your fingers to bend the ends so that the ring looks like Figure 10.

4. Using the round-nosed pliers, loop each end. See Figure 1 for the exact shape of the loops.

5. Bend the loops back and into place as in Figure 1.

6. Apply a finish of your choice.

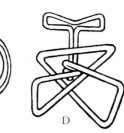

A   B   C   D

Figure 1

BUTTONS AND CUFF LINKS

THESE DESIGNS FOR BUTTONS MAY also be used for cuff links by adding extra links to the other side. D in Figure 1 shows one kind of extra link, Figure 7 shows another.

TO MAKE THE BUTTON LETTERED A IN FIGURE 1

YOU WILL NEED:

5 inches (12.5 cm) of 14-gauge wire.

1. Cut a 5-inch (12.5 cm) length of 14-gauge wire. File both ends round.

2. Hold the wire in the tip of the round-nosed pliers at a point 2 1/4 inches (5.5 cm) from one end of the wire. Make a loop like the one in Figure 2. The point marked A shows where the pliers grip the wire.

3. Coil the short end of the wire to fit Figure 3.

4. Coil the other end to fit Figure 1 A.

5. Apply a finish of your choice.

HOW TO MAKE A PAIR OF CUFF LINKS USING BUTTONS

Make two buttons like the one Lettered A in Figure 1 following the directions above. Or make two buttons each from the designs for the buttons lettered B or C in Figure 1.

NOTE: You can also use almost any buttons you have on hand if they have a shank to which you can attach the second link.

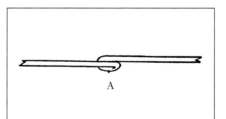

A

Figure 2

YOU WILL NEED:

8 inches (20.5 cm) of 16-gauge wire

1. Cut two lengths of 16-gauge wire, each 4 inches (10 cm) long.

File one end of each length round, the other flat.

2. Using the tip of the round-nosed pliers, loop the flat end of each length, making small loops like the one in Figure 4.

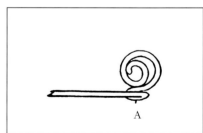

A

Figure 3

3. Using the parallel or flat-nosed pliers, bend each length to make a right angle like the one in Figure 4.

4. Hold the loop of one of the lengths in your left hand. Using your finger, bend the wire into a circle about the size of a shirt button, keeping it at a right angle to the loop, as in Figure 5.

5. Using the round-nosed pliers, curve the end of the wire around and bring it inside the first circle, tucking it in as shown in Figure 6. Repeat these steps on the other unit.

6. Open the loop of each unit sideways.

7. Apply a finish of your choice.

8. Assemble the cuff links as shown in Figure 7.

TO MAKE THE BUTTON LETTERED B IN FIGURE 1

YOU WILL NEED:

6 inches (15 cm) of 14-gauge wire

Approximately 25 inches (63.5 cm) of 18-gauge wire

A mandrel 5/32 inch (3.75 mm) in diameter, the approximate size of a #5 (US) knitting needle

1. Cut a length of 14-gauge wire 6 inches (15 cm) long. File both ends round.

2. Using the round-nosed pliers, hold the wire at the center point. Loop the wire as shown in Figure 8. Be sure the ends cross each other in the right way.

3. Hold this loop in the parallel or flat-nosed pliers. With the lower end of wire, use your fingers to form another larger loop at a right

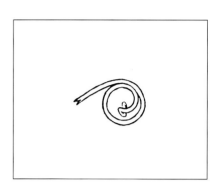

Figure 4

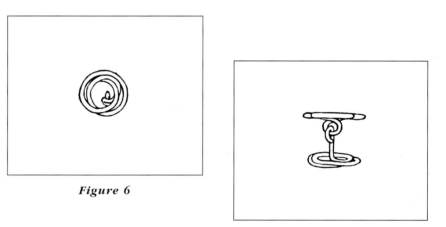

Figure 5

Figure 6

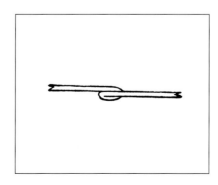

Figure 7

Figure 8

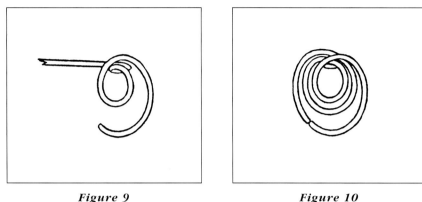

Figure 9	*Figure 10*

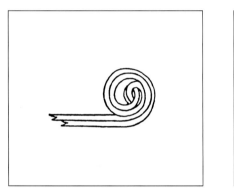

Figure 11

Figure 12

angle to the first. Continue the curve around the outside of this loop until the unit looks like Figure 9.

4. Continue holding the first loop in the parallel or flat-nosed pliers and curve the other end so that the unit looks like Figure 10. Be sure that this end of wire passes under the other, and not over it.

5. Wrap 42 rounds of 18-gauge wire around the mandrel (#5 (US) knitting needle). Remove the spring from the mandrel, cut it free, and trim the end.

6. Using your fingers, bend the spring into a half-circle. Be careful to bend it evenly—do not open the rounds more in one spot than in another.

7. Open the largest circle of the 14-gauge unit in the same way you would open a jump ring by bending one end a little to the side to make enough room to slide the 18-gauge spring onto one of the ends.

8. Slide the spring onto the 14-gauge unit, compressing it to get the last part of the 14-gauge circle inside of it.

9. Push the large circle of the 14-gauge unit closed, letting the spring slip up into place (see Figure 1 B).

10. With the tip of the round-nosed pliers, grasp one end of the 18-gauge unit. Pull the end of the wire around and around to make the last few rounds smaller and tapered, as in Figure 1 B.

11. Using the parallel or flat-nosed pliers, tuck the end in behind the 14-gauge wire, pressing it out of the way against the back of the heaver wire.

12. Apply a finish of your choice.

TO MAKE THE BUTTON LETTERED C IN FIGURE 1

YOU WILL NEED:

9 inches (23 cm) of 14-gauge wire.

1. Cut a 9-inch (23 cm) length of 14-gauge wire. File both ends round.

2. Loop the length of wire in the center as you did for the first button (Figure 2).

3. Hold the loop in the round-nosed pliers. Using your fingers, pull the ends around in a clockwise direction, as in Figure 11.

4. Bend both ends of the wire around to make the button shown in Figure 1 C, and in a side view in Figure 12. Keep the round close together and let the inner round overlap the outer ones a bit. Make sure that the loop extends down below the button far enough for easy sewing.

5. Using the round-nosed pliers, tuck the ends up inside the button.

6. Apply a finish of your choice.

TO MAKE CUFF LINKS LIKE D IN FIGURE 1

YOU WILL NEED:

11 1/2 inches (29 cm) of 14-gauge wire

6 inches (15 cm) of 16-gauge wire

1. Cut two lengths of 14-gauge wire, each 5 3/4 inches (14.5 cm) long.

File both ends of each length round.

2. Loop both ends of each length. The loops should be absolutely round, and have an inside diameter of at least 1/8 inch (3 mm).

3. Using the parallel or flat-nosed pliers, bend each length to fit Figure 1 D. Be sure the wire crosses over and under itself correctly. Compare your work with Figure 1 D before you make each angle. (If you find it difficult to make the angles sharp, refer to Chapter Two, page 21.)

4. Cut two lengths of 16-gauge wire, each 3 inches (7.5 cm) long.

File all the ends round.

5. Using the parallel or flat-nosed pliers, bend each length to fit Figure 13, then Figure 14, then Figure 15, then Figure 16.

6. Loop both ends of each unit in the same direction.

7. Open the loops, one to one side, the other to the other side.

Assemble by inserting these loops into the loops of the cuff links (see Figure 1 D).

8. Apply a finish of your choice.

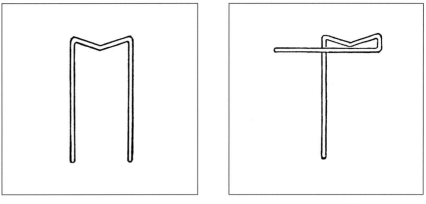

Figure 13

Figure 14

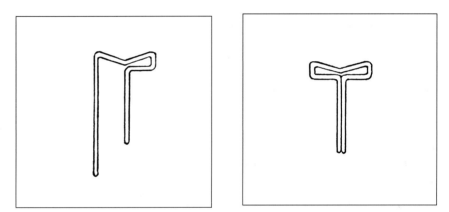

Figure 15

Figure 16

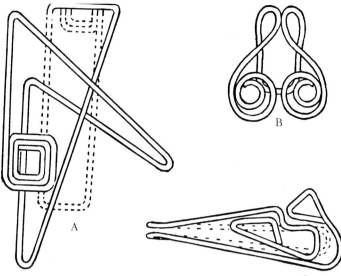

Figure 1

CLIPS

THESE PAPER CLIPS ARE EASY-TO- make decorative accessories. You can use one as a book mark and one as a tie clip.

The clip principle is so simple that you can use almost any kind of design that shows in front. While you don't want to cross the wire over itself too many times, you'll need to make sure the top part crosses the part that goes behind the paper (or tie) at least in enough places so it will hold firmly.

TO MAKE THE PAPER CLIP LETTERED A IN FIGURE 1

YOU WILL NEED:

22 1/2 inches (57 cm) of 14-gauge wire.

1. Cut a 22 1/2-inch (57 cm) length of 14-gauge wire. File both ends flat.

2. Using the parallel or flat-nosed pliers, bend the ends of the wire to fit Figure 2. (See Chapter Two, page 21, on how to make angles, and Chapter 10, page 49, on how to get the rounds of wire close to each other.)

3. Using the parallel pliers, bend the wire to fit Figure 1 A. Figure 3 shows the shape of a clip as it looks from the side. This is the shape that every clip should have so that it will slide easily.

4. Pound the clip. This is very important. Pounding gives a clip spring. You can pound the various parts as you go along before you cross the wire over itself. Use your own judgment in selecting the pounding tool based on the finished look you want for the piece.

Use a soft mallet where you wish to avoid marks or too much flattening.

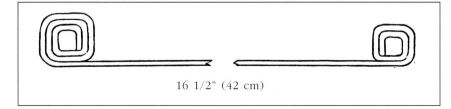

16 1/2" (42 cm)

Figure 2

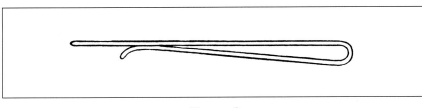

Figure 3

Or, use a hard hammer where the marks and flattening will add to the attractiveness of the piece.

5. Apply a finish of your choice.

TO MAKE THE PAPER CLIP LETTERED B IN FIGURE 1

This clip also makes a good book mark. You can easily use other design motifs in place of the coils.

YOU WILL NEED:

8 1/2 inches (21.5 cm) of 14-gauge wire.

1. Cut an 8 1/2-inch (21.5 cm) length of 14-gauge wire.

File the ends round.

2. Using the round-nosed pliers, coil the ends to fit Figure 4.

3. To make the coils, you will need to find the point where you will hold the unit in the round-nosed pliers. To do this, place one of the coils over Figure 1 B.

4. Bend the unit to fit Figure 1 B. Repeat with the other coil, bending the center so that the loops touch each other as in Figure 1 B.

5. Pound the wire to stiffen it and give the clip spring.

6. Apply a finish of your choice.

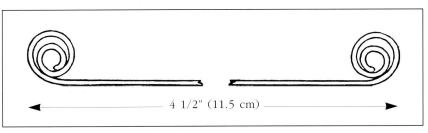

4 1/2" (11.5 cm)

Figure 4

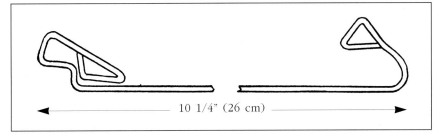

10 1/4" (26 cm)

Figure 5

TO MAKE THE PAPER CLIP LETTERED C IN FIGURE 1

This design also makes a nice tie clip.

YOU WILL NEED:

12 inches (30.5 cm) of 14-gauge wire.

1. Cut a 12-inch (30.5 cm) length of 14-gauge wire. File the ends flat.

2. Using the parallel or flat-nosed pliers to make the angles, and your fingers to make the curve, bend the ends to fit Figure 5.

3. Using your fingers, bend the wire so that the two ends come together as in Figure 1 C.

4. Pound the unit to give it spring.

5. Using the round-nosed pliers, shape the back part of the clip, bending it as shown in Figure 1 C.

6. Apply a finish of your choice.

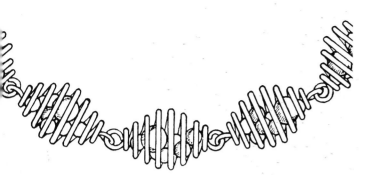

Figure 1

19
CHAPTER

BIRD CAGES

YOU CAN FILL THESE CAGES WITH almost anything you happen to have on hand. Small shells, rock chips, beads, or pieces from an old necklace will add interest and color.

YOU WILL NEED:

132 inches (3.3 m) of 16-gauge wire

Beads or other findings to fit in the cages. To give you an estimate of what you'll need, the piece illustrated in Figure 1 uses 91 5 mm balls, and 13 9/32-inch (6 mm) balls.

1. Cut 13 lengths of 16-gauge wire, each 10 inches (25.5 cm) long.

File all the ends flat.

2. Loop one end of each length of wire, bending the loop over a bit as shown in Figure 2.

3. Hold one of the lengths in the parallel or flat-nosed pliers, as shown in Figure 3. Press your left thumb against the wire where it emerges from the pliers. Coil the wire into a circle that lies flat against the pliers as in Figure 4. Coil the wire around the outside of this circle, and continue to bend it around the coil until it looks like Figure 5. Stop coiling when the free end of wire measures 5 inches (12.5 cm). Repeat these steps on the other lengths.

4. Loop the other end of each unit. Be sure the loop lies in the same plane as the first loop as shown in Figure 6.

5. Bend the looped end of each unit into a circle, then a coil, just as you did the other ends. With the loops pointing up toward you, measure each unit against Figure 7 by placing the unit on the drawing.

6. Using your fingers, bend each unit at the center point so that the two coils are flat against each other and the loops extend in opposite directions on each side of the unit as in Figure 8.

7. Hold one of the units in your left hand. Using the tip of the round-nosed pliers as a wedge, open up a space between the coils. Slide the tip of the pliers around between the rounds of the coil, forcing the flat coil to become an open spiral, as shown in Figure 9. The spiral will be even all the way to the end if you keep the tip of the pliers inserted to the same point while exerting a steady pressure. When you reach the end of the spiral, you will have to grasp the last circle with the pliers and pry it up a bit so the unit looks like Figure 10.

Figure 2

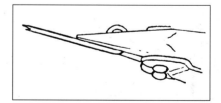

Figure 3

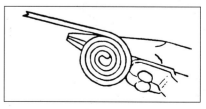

Figure 4

Figure 5

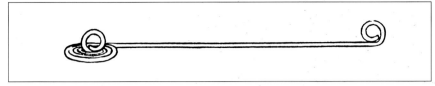

Figure 6

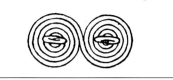

Figure 7

Figure 8

Figure 9

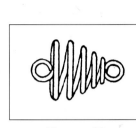

Figure 10

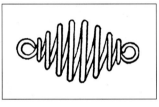

Figure 11

Open the other coil of that unit, and the coils on each end of the other units, to make 13 units like Figure 11. Open the loop at one end of each of the cages sideways.

8. For a hook, cut one length of 16-gauge wire 2 inches (5 cm) long. File one end flat, the other round. Make a hook like the one in Chapter Three on page 24. Open its loop sideways.

9. Assemble the necklace as shown in Figure 1 with the hook on one end.

10. Apply a finish of your choice.

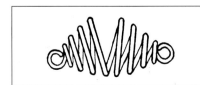

Figure 12

11. After the lacquer has dried, use your fingers to open each unit at a point somewhere near the center as in Figure 12. Insert the findings of your choice, and close the units with your fingers.

HOW TO MAKE EARRINGS TO MATCH THE NECKLACE

YOU WILL NEED:

28 inches (71 cm) of 16-gauge wire

14 5-mm balls,

2 9/32-inch (6 mm) balls

A pair of earring backs

Household cement or liquid solder

1. Cut two lengths of 16-gauge wire, each one 10 inches (25.5 cm) long.

2. Make two cages like the ones you made for the necklace.

3. Cut the loop from one end of each cage.

4. Cut two lengths of 16-gauge wire, each 4 inches (10 cm) long.

File one end flat.

5. Make two coiled units from which to hang the cage units as shown in Figure 13. (The procedure follows the same principle as the directions in Chapter One, here using heavier wire.)

6. Stop coiling each unit when there is about 1/2 inch (1.5 cm) of wire left extending beyond the coil.

7. Loop the 1/2-inch (1.5 cm) ends back as shown in Figure 13. Open the loops on these coiled units sideways.

8. Assemble the earrings as shown in Figure 13.

9. Apply a finish of your choice.

10. After the lacquer dries, open the cage units as you did the ones in the necklace. Insert the balls or beads, and close the units.

11. Using household cement or liquid solder, attach the commercial earring backs to the coiled units.

Figure 13

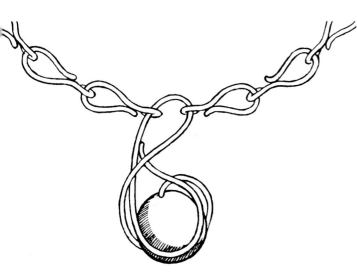

Figure 1

20
CHAPTER

CHAIN WITH PENDANT

THE PENDANT FOR THIS NECKLACE is just one of the many possible shapes you can create for holding a large ball. Once you understand the mechanics, you can experiment to make pendants of other shapes.

For this design, the ball is held by two curves and a point—three firm points of contact are all that is needed. The curves have been squeezed together and then released to put some spring into them.

YOU WILL NEED:
---

51 inches (1.3 m) of 14-gauge wire

A marble or ball 5/8 inch (1.6 cm) or 3/4 inch (2 cm) in diameter (3/4 inch (2 cm) shown in Figure 1)

1. Cut 21 lengths of 14-gauge wire, each 2 inches (5 cm) long.

File one end of each length flat, the other round. Loop the flat end of each length.

2. Make 10 links to fit the link to the left of the pendant in Figure 1, and 11 links to fit the one to the right. Leave the last link open at the end to make a hook.

3. Open all the loops sideways.

4. Cut a jump ring from the spring made for Chapter Three, or one like it (see page 22 for directions). Open the jump ring, and file its ends flat.

5. Cut one length of 14-gauge wire 8 inches (20.5 cm) long to make the pendant. File the ends round.

6. Using your fingers, loop one end in a large, oval loop the shape of the one that lies on top of the ball in Figure 1.

7. Bend the wire back to form the loop to which the chain links are attached.

8. Hold the marble or ball in place where it will be when assembled, then bend the wire around behind it, using your fingers. Press the end of the wire firmly against the ball at

a point half way between the two curves of wire. Use the round-nosed pliers if you find them helpful. Remove the ball.

9. Assemble the necklace so there are two chains of 10 links on each side, with the pendant in the center. The links should be alternated as in Figure 1. The hook goes on the end that is held in the right hand as the necklace is put on, the jump ring goes on the other end.

10. Apply a finish of your choice.

11. After the lacquer dries, insert the ball or marble and squeeze the curves of wire to hold the ball firmly in place.

Figure 1

LOOP-THE-LOOP

IN THIS SET OF MATCHING NECKLACE, bracelet, and earrings, we use a half-ball that is held in place by loops of wire at the center of each link. You can also use a flat button in place of the half-ball.

HOW TO MAKE A NECKLACE OF THIS DESIGN

YOU WILL NEED:

114 1/2 inches (2.8 m) of 16-gauge wire

Nine half-balls 5/8 inch (1.6 cm) in diameter, or nine buttons of the same size.

1. Cut nine lengths of 16-gauge wire, each 11 inches (28 cm) long. If you have found some buttons you want to use but do not have nine of them, cut as many 11-inch (28 cm) lengths as you have buttons. You can add more of the smaller units later to fill out the length of the necklace.

File all the ends flat.

2. Using the round-nosed pliers, hold one of the lengths at a point 1/2 inch (1.5 cm) from one end.

3. Using your fingers, bend the long end of the wire around the base of the pliers as shown in Figure 2.

4. To complete the loop, shift the grip of your pliers to the other side of the loop as shown in Figure 3.

5. Make eight loops, each one almost, but not quite, touching the ones on either side of it. Compare each loop with Figure 4 as you complete it. (You may find it hard to get the loops even at first, but a bit of practice will soon make you an expert.) There will be 1 1/2 inches (4 cm) of wire left when you have made eight loops.

Repeat these steps on each of the 11-inch (28 cm) lengths of wire, frequently comparing each one with Figure 4.

6. Hold one of the units in your fingers as shown in Figure 5.

Press the first loop away from you, and at the same time press the second loop toward you, so that the unit looks like Figure 6.

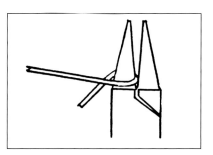

Figure 2

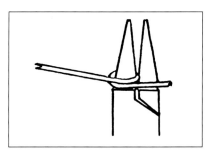

Figure 3

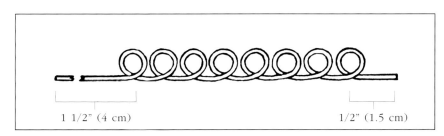

1 1/2" (4 cm)   1/2" (1.5 cm)

Figure 4

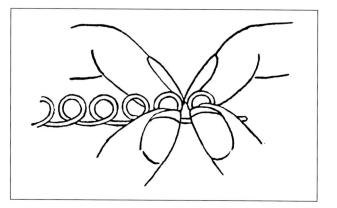

Figure 5

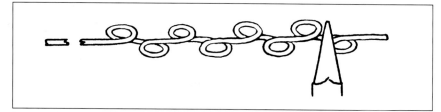

Figure 6

Figure 7

7. Press each loop in the same way, so that the unit has alternating loops bent in opposite directions, and looks like Figure 7. Repeat these steps on the other units.

8. Hold one of the units in the round-nosed pliers with the loops pointing away from you, as in Figure 7.

9. Bend the unit, using your fingers, so that there is a slight curve between the first and second loops. Bend the unit in the same way between each of the loops, so that when you have bent it seven times it will fit Figure 8. Repeat these steps on each unit.

10. Using the round-nosed pliers, loop the 1/2-inch (1.5 cm) end of each unit so that it looks like Figure 9.

11. Again, use the round-nosed pliers to loop the 1 1/2-inch (4 cm) end of each unit twice so it fits Figure 10.

12. Open the single loop on the shorter end of each unit sideways.

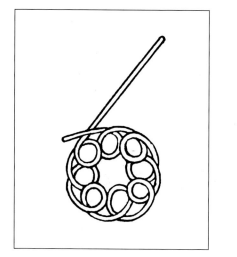

Figure 8

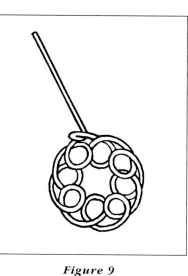

Figure 9

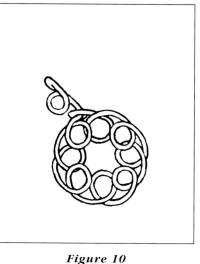

Figure 10

Close the loop of each unit around the other end of the wire, as shown in Figure 10.

13. Cut six lengths of 16-gauge wire, each 2 inches (5 cm) long.

NOTE: (Each of these lengths will make a unit that will add approximately 1/2 (1.5 cm) inch to the length of the necklace. If you did not make nine of the large units, you must make more of these smaller ones, according to the length required.

File all the ends flat.

14. Loop one end of each unit as shown in Figure 11. Next, loop each unit to fit Figure 12, then to fit Figure 13.

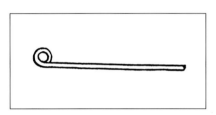

Figure 11

15. Open the loops on the free end of each of the large, round units, and on the left end of each of the small units.

16. For the hook, cut one length of 16-gauge wire 2 inches (5 cm) long. File one end flat, the other round. Make a hook like the one in Chapter Three on page 24. Open its loop.

17. Cut a jump ring from the spring made for Chapter Three (see page 22 if you do not have a spring). Open the jump ring sideways, and file its ends flat.

18. Assemble the necklace by connecting the large units as shown in Figure 1, with three small units added to each end, plus the hook

on one end and the jump ring on the other.

19. Apply a finish of your choice.

20. Insert the nine half-balls or the buttons into the large units after the necklace has dried. As you can see in Figure 1, alternating loops go over and under the half-balls. You will probably have to pry up the four loops that go on top in order to get the half-ball or button inside, then press them down again. Since pliers would scar the finish, try to press the loops down firmly enough with your fingers.

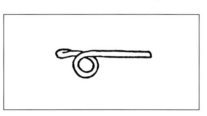

Figure 12

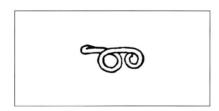

Figure 13

HOW TO MAKE A MATCHING BRACELET

YOU WILL NEED:

67 1/2 inches (1.7 m) of 16-gauge wire

Five half-balls 5/8 inch (1.6 cm) in diameter, or five buttons of the same size.

1. Cut five lengths of 16-gauge wire, each 11 inches (28 cm) long.

2. Make five units just like the ones you made for the necklace. Do not loop the free end of the last unit you make. Leave it looking like Figure 9, on page 86.

3. Bend the free end of this last unit to fit the unit lettered C in Figure 14. This is the eye into which the hook fits.

4. Cut four lengths of 16-gauge wire, each 2 inches (5 cm) long.

File the ends flat.

Make four units like the one lettered A in Figure 14. Open the loops on each end of the small units sideways.

5. For the hook, cut a 4 1/2-inch (11.5 cm) length of 16-gauge wire.

File the ends flat. Make a hook like the one lettered B in Figure 14, opening its loops sideways.

6. Assemble the bracelet in this order: the five large units attach to one another in a series with the

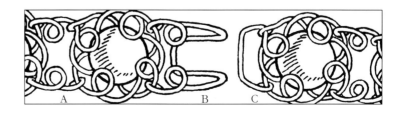

Figure 14

fifth one, which has the eye on it, at the left end of the series (see Figure 14 for the exact spot where the loop of one circles the edge of the next); the four small units go between the large units (again, see Figure 14); and the hook goes on the right end of the series.

7. Apply a finish of your choice.

8. Insert the half-balls or buttons into the large units after the bracelet is dry, following the directions for the necklace.

HOW TO MAKE MATCHING EARRINGS

YOU WILL NEED:

20 1/2 inches (52 cm) of 16-gauge wire

Two half-balls 5/8 inch (1.6 cm) in diameter, or two buttons of the same size

Two commercial earring backs.

Household cement or liquid solder

1. Cut two lengths of 16-gauge wire, each 10 1/4 inches (26 cm) long.

2. Make two units like the ones you made for the necklace to hold the buttons or half-balls.

NOTE: The end that extends beyond the body of the earring unit is shorter than the end that extends from the necklace unit. This leaves only enough to make the small loop at the bottom of the earring unit (see Figure 15).

Figure 15

3. Apply a finish of your choice.

4. Insert the half-balls or buttons after the earrings are dry, as you did for the necklace.

5. Using the household cement or liquid solder, attach a commercial earring back to each earring.

Figure 1

COLORFUL DANGLES

USE TINY BEADS OR THE SMALLEST pearls from an old necklace to enhance these dangles. A 5-mm ball or bead will also fit. If you do use beads, be careful to insert them to conceal the hole through the center.

YOU WILL NEED:

Approximately 200 inches (5 m) of 18-gauge wire .

A mandrel 5/32 inch (3.75 mm) in diameter, approximately the size of a #5 (US) knitting needle

42 balls, beads, or pearls, 6 mm in diameter

1. Wind 18-gauge wire around the mandrel (#5 (US) knitting needle) to make 329 complete rounds (see Chapter One, page 15). Remove the spring from the mandrel and, if necessary, cut it from the spool or coil. Trim the ends.

2. From this spring, cut:

7 units of 23 rounds each

36 units of 4 rounds each

2 units of 12 rounds each

3. Using the round-nosed pliers, loop one end of each 23-round unit as shown in Figure 2.

4. Hold one of the looped units in your left hand with the loop to the right. Insert the tip of the round-nosed pliers between the third and fourth rounds to open the space between these two rounds as shown in Figure 3. If you have sturdy fingernails, you may find it easier to use a thumbnail than the pliers.

5. Continue to open spaces as you did in Step 4 between rounds in five more places to make a unit that looks like Figure 4. Repeat these steps on the other 23-round units.

6. Using the round-nosed pliers, bend the last two rounds of each unit upward at a right angle. Loop the end as shown in Figure 5.

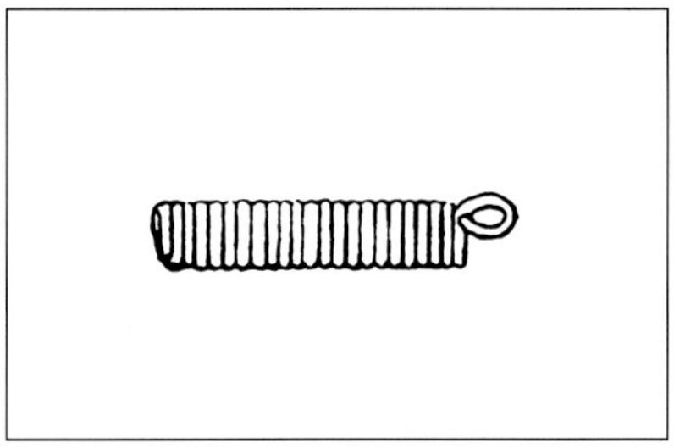

7. Using the parallel or flat-nosed pliers, open the smaller loop that you made first as shown in Figure 5. Using the round-nosed pliers, pull the opened loop around so you can close it around the shank of the larger loop as shown in Figure 6.

8. Make 36 units for the chain from the four-round units you have cut. Make them the same way you made the chain in Chapter 14. Refer to Figures 4 and 5 and the detailed directions for that chain on page 68. Open the round on one end of these units sideways.

9. Assemble the 36 units into a chain, inserting the opened loop of

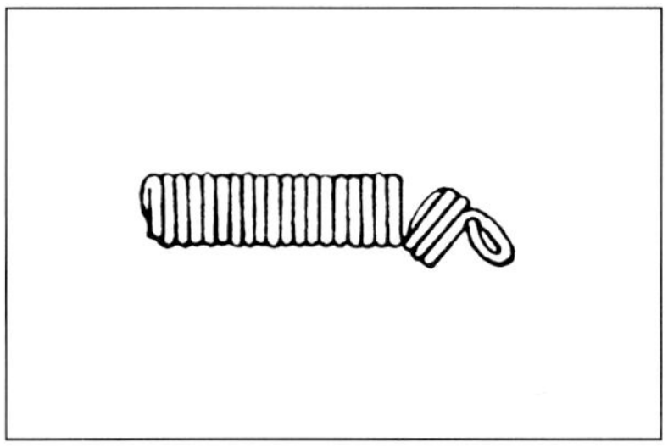

Figure 2

Figure 3

Figure 4

Figure 5

Figure 6

Figure 7

each unit through the closed loop of the next, then closing the opened loop.

10. Make a hook-and-eye clasp from the two 12-round units already cut. See Chapter 14, page 68, Figures 6 and 7, for detailed instructions.

11. Attach the large 23-round units to the chain as shown in Figure 1. The first large unit hangs from the ninth link of the chain. the rest hang from every third link, leaving nine links on the other end to balance.

12. Apply a finish of your choice.

13. Insert the beads, pearls, or balls after the necklace is dry, as shown in Figure 1. If the units have been made well (the openings should all be the same size and the units should not be twisted, but all lie in the same plane) each ball will pop into place with only a little pressure. It should not fall out again under normal conditions.

HOW TO MAKE MATCHING EARRINGS

YOU WILL NEED:

32 inches (81.5 cm) of 18-gauge wire

12 6-mm balls or beads

Two commercial earring backs

Household cement or liquid solder

1. Cut two lengths of 18-gauge wire, each 3 1/2 inches (9 cm) long.

File the ends flat.

2. Coil each length, looping its end to fit Figure 7. (Refer to Chapter 19, page 83).

3. Wind 46 complete rounds of 18-gauge wire around the same mandrel (#5 (US) knitting needle) you used for the necklace. Remove the spring and cut two units of 23 rounds each.

4. Make two units like the ones you made for the necklace (Figures 2-6).

5. Assemble the earrings as shown in Figure 7, but without the balls.

6. Apply a finish of your choice.

7. After the earrings are dry, insert the balls or beads as you did with the necklace units. Attach the commercial earring backs.

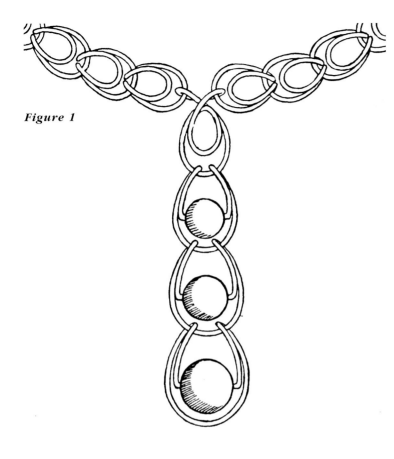

Figure 1

TRIPLE PENDANT

THIS VERSATILE DESIGN ALLOWS YOU to use several beads of graduated sizes. If you want to use more beads (or less), it's easy to change the number of links in the center dangle to accommodate any amount you desire. You can also vary the size of the links in the dangle and earrings if you have beads that aren't quite the same size as those shown here. We adapted the chain from a practical one we purchased in a hardware store--an example that you can find good design anywhere.

YOU WILL NEED:

---

101 3/4 inches (2.5 m) of 16-gauge wire

3 1/2 inches (9 cm) of 14-gauge wire

Three beads of graduated sizes (about 3/8 inch (1 cm), 1/2 inch (1.5 cm), and 5/8 inch (1.6 cm) in diameter)

1. Cut 28 lengths of 16-gauge wire, each 3 inches (7.5 cm) long.

File all the ends round.

2. Using the round-nosed pliers, bend each length to fit Figure 2, measuring each one against the figure.

3. Again, using the round-nosed pliers, bend each unit to fit Figure 3, then Figure 4, then Figure 5. Figure 6 shows how each unit should look from the side when it has reached the stage shown in Figure 5.

4. Cut one length of 16-gauge wire 4 3/4 inches (12 cm) long.

File the ends round.

5. Using the tip of the round-nosed pliers, loop both ends to make loops that are perfectly round and large enough for 16-gauge wire to slip through them easily.

6. Using the round-nosed pliers, bend the length to fit Figure 7.

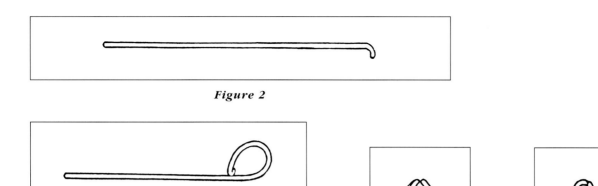

Figure 2

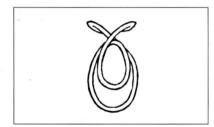

Figure 3

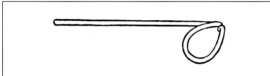

Figure 4

Figure 5

Figure 6

Figure 7

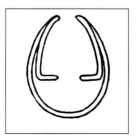

Figure 8

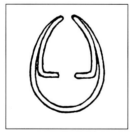

Figure 9

Figure 10

7. Using the parallel or flat-nosed pliers, open both loops of this unit sideways.

8. To make the three units of the center pendant, cut one length of 16-gauge wire 3 3/4 inches (9.5 cm) long, one length 4 1/4 inches (11 cm) long, and one length 5 inches (12.5 cm) long.

9. Using the round-nosed pliers, bend the 3 3/4-inch (9.5 cm) length to fit Figure 8. Next, bend the 4 1/4-inch (11 cm) length to fit Figure 9. Then bend the 5-inch (12.5 cm) length to fit Figure 10.

10. For the hook, cut one length of 14-gauge wire 2 inches (5 cm) long. File one end round, the other flat. Make a hook like the one in Chapter Three, page 24, Figure 12.

11. Cut a 14-gauge jump ring from the spring made for Chapter Three, or make one according to the directions on page 22 if you do not have a spring left.

12. Assemble the necklace without the beads. Fourteen of the small units make a chain for each side of the necklace, with the 4 3/4-inch (12 cm) length (Figure 7) joining them, as shown in Figure 1. To link the small units together, pass the smaller loop of one unit through the larger loop of the next unit from behind. Using your fingers, press the smaller loop of the first unit down flat so that the two units will not come apart. The larger units for the pendant are attached as shown in Figure 1.

13. Apply a finish of your choice.

14. Insert the beads in the pendant units after the necklace is dry.

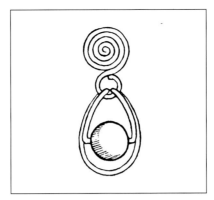

Figure 11

HOW TO MAKE MATCHING EARRINGS

You will need:

15 1/2 inches (39.5 cm) of 16-gauge wire

Two beads

Two commercial earring backs.

Household cement or liquid solder

1. Cut two lengths of 16-gauge wire 3 3/4 inches (9.5 cm) long.

File the ends round.

2. Make two units to fit Figure 11, following the same method you used to make the necklace units.

3. Cut two lengths of 16-gauge wire each 4 inches (10 cm) long.

File one end of each length flat.

4. Coil these lengths to make two units like the top unit in Figure 11.

5. Assemble the earrings as shown in Figure 11.

6. Apply a finish of your choice.

7. When the earrings are dry, insert the beads as you did for the necklace pendant.

8. Using household cement or liquid solder, attach the commercial earring backs.

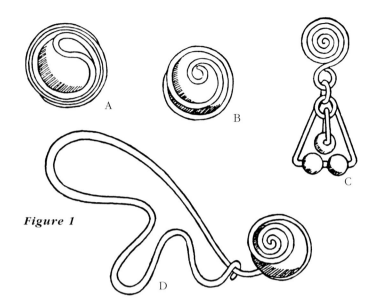

A FEW EXTRAS

Figure 1

WHETHER IT'S A LARGE RING WITH dramatic flair, cuff links, earrings, or a key ring, you'll find these accessories make great gifts. Use beads or stones you already have, using the leftovers from other projects.

TO MAKE THE RING LETTERED A IN FIGURE 1

YOU WILL NEED:

15 inches (38 cm) of 14-gauge wire

A half-ball 3/4 inch (2 cm) in diameter, or any stone you may want to use of approximately the same size

1. Cut a 15-inch (38 cm) length of 14-gauge wire.

File the ends round.

2. Loop the wire in the center to fit Figure 2, and curve the ends around as shown.

3. Holding the unit in parallel or flat-nosed pliers as shown in Figure 3, bend the loop up so that the inner round of wire and the part of the loop marked A in Figure 2 are higher than the rest of the unit. This will make the loop fit the curve of the half-ball you will place under it.

4. Bend both ends of the wire around to fit Figure 4. Let the inner rounds overlap the outer rounds a bit so that the ring will be raised in the center (see the ring directions on page 74, Step 3).

5. To start the part of the ring that goes around the finger, bend the ends to make right angles to the part you just made in Step 4.

6. To form the part of the ring that circles the wearer's finger, use your fingers to bend the ends around. Make two rounds, the tops of which should come up just a bit under the outer rim of the design already made.

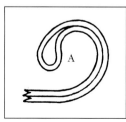

Figure 2

Figure 3

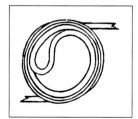

Figure 4

7. Loop each end, then bend the loops up under the top of the ring so they'll press upward against the half-ball when it's inserted between them and the top design. Figure 5 shows how the ring should look from the top after completing this step.

8. Apply a finish of your choice.

9. After the ring is dry, use your fingers to open the ring by bending the rounds that circle the finger away from the design that lies on top of the finger. Insert the half-ball, then close the ring again. (Do not use pliers for this step since they will mar the lacquer.)

TO MAKE THE BUTTON LETTERED B IN FIGURE 1

YOU WILL NEED:

7 inches (18 cm) of 14-gauge wire

A half-ball 3/4 inch (2 cm) in diameter

NOTE: This design can be used for any size half-ball by altering the number of inches of wire used or by using 16-gauge wire instead of the thicker 14-gauge.

1. Cut a 7-inch (18 cm) length of 14-gauge wire.

File one end round, the other flat.

2. Loop the rounded end and measure it against the center loop in Figure 6. Next, coil the wire to fit Figure 6. Then loop the free end of the wire.

3. Place the coiled portion of the unit over the half-ball. Use your fingers to press it into a gradual spiral that fits closely over the ball. The last complete round should circle the edge of the half-ball.

4. Coil the end of the wire so it will hold the half-ball in place as

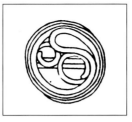

Figure 5

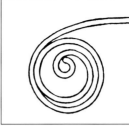

Figure 6

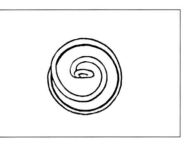

Figure 7

shown in Figure 7 which is the back view of the button.

5. Remove the half-ball and bend the last circle away from it with your fingers.

6. Apply a finish of your choice.

7. Insert the half-ball after the lacquer is dry. Using your fingers, press the wire back into place.

TO MAKE THE EARRING LETTERED C IN FIGURE 1

YOU WILL NEED:

17 inches (43 cm) of 16-gauge wire

Six small beads approximately 1/4 inch (6.3 mm) in diameter.

A mandrel 5/32 inch (3.7 mm) in diameter, approximately the size of a #5 (US) knitting needle

1. Cut two lengths of 16-gauge wire, each 1 inch (2.5 cm) long.

File the ends flat.

2. Using the parallel or flat-nosed pliers, bend each length to fit Figure 8.

3. Cut two lengths of 16-gauge wire, each 2 1/4 inches (5.5 cm) long. File the ends flat.

4. Bend each length to fit Figure 9.

5. Cut two lengths of 16-gauge wire, each 4 inches (10 cm) long.

File one end of each length flat.

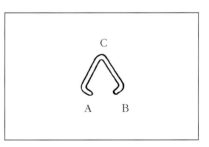

Figure 8

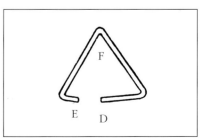

Figure 9

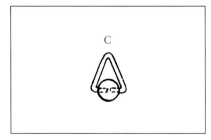

Figure 10

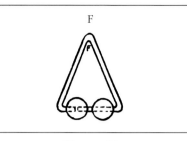

Figure 11

6. Coil the other end of each length to make two units that look like the top unit in Figure 1 C .

7. Wind 16-gauge wire around the mandrel (#5 (US) knitting needle) to make at least four jump rings. Cut four jump rings, open them sideways, and file their ends flat.

8. Assemble the earrings as shown in Figure 1 C without the beads.

9. Apply a finish of your choice.

10. Add the beads as shown in Figures 10 and 11.

TO MAKE THE KEY RING LETTERED D IN FIGURE 1

YOU WILL NEED:

13 1/2 inches (34 cm) of 14-gauge wire

A ball 5/8 inch (1.6 cm) in diameter, or a marble of about the same size

1. Cut a 13 1/2-inch (34 cm) length of 14-gauge wire.

File the ends round.

2. Coil one end to fit the coil on the top of the ball in Figure 1 D.

3. Hold this coil on the top of the ball. Pull the wire around the ball in a spiral shape, ending with a complete circle on the opposite side of the ball from the first coil.

4. Using your fingers, form the rest of the key ring to fit Figure 1 D.

5. Open the coil with your fingers, and remove the ball from the spiral.

6. Use a steel hammer to pound the large loops of wire. This will put enough "spring" into the key ring while flattening it.

7. To put even more spring into it, pull the hook away from the wire it hooks to.

8. Apply a finish of your choice.

9. After the lacquer is dry, insert the ball and close the spiral around it.

Figure 1

VARIATIONS OF THE EGYPTIAN

THE TECHNIQUES IN THIS CHAPTER should be familiar to you since the designs are all variations on the Egyptian coil. Its popularity has spanned thousands of years, inspiring artisans throughout the ages. We continue to find this design endlessly fascinating—perhaps that's why it's been around for so long.

Some of the variations that are suitable for bracelets or necklaces are shown in Figure 1. Later on in the chapter, you'll find suggestions for a ring, earrings, another bracelet, and another necklace.

NOTE: The instructions are much less detailed than for the previous chapters. By now you should know the principles involved and can adapt them to any necessary changes. We will continue to show illustrations for any complicated procedures.

TO MAKE THE BRACELET LETTERED A IN FIGURE 1

YOU WILL NEED:

199 inches (5 m) of 18-gauge wire. This will make a 7 1/2-inch (19 cm) bracelet.

1 inch (2.5 cm) of 16-gauge wire

A mandrel about 9/32 inch (6.5 mm) in diameter, approximately the size of a #15 or #16 (US) knitting needle

1. Cut 32 lengths of 18-gauge wire, each 6 inches (15 cm) long.

2. Make and assemble the bracelet according to the directions in Chapter 10, on page 50.

3. Use the tip of the parallel pliers to make the first angles, and measure your work against the drawing marked A in Figure 1 instead of the drawings in Chapter 10.

4. Use a 7-inch (18 cm) length of 18-gauge wire for the hook, and 16-gauge wire for the jump ring.

TO MAKE THE BRACELET LETTERED B IN FIGURE 1

YOU WILL NEED:

271 inches (6.7 m) of 18-gauge wire

1 inch (2.5 cm) of 16-gauge wire

1. Cut 35 lengths of 18-gauge wire 7 1/2 inches (19 cm) long, and cut one length 8 1/2 inches (21.5 cm) long.

2. Coil both ends of each of the 7 1/2-inch (19 cm) lengths, following the directions in Chapter One, page 14, until each unit measures 2 inches (5 cm) overall.

3. Bend each unit as shown in Chapter One, Figures 13 and 14, on page 14, and then as shown in Figures 15 and 16 on the same page. These units should be bent exactly in the middle when the unit reaches the stage shown in Chapter One, Figure 16. Both the loop and the coiled portion should measure almost 1/2 inch (1.5 cm).

X

Figure 2

Figure 3

Figure 4

4. Assemble the bracelet. In this case, you will find the assembling a bit more complicated. First, flatten one unit and pull the two coils slightly apart. Insert the loop of the second unit down through the loop of the first, pull its coils apart, and slip the coils under the coils of the first unit (see Figure 2). Insert the loop of the third unit down through the loops of both the first and second units. The X marked in Figure 2 shows where to insert the loop. Figure 3 shows the three units as the third is being inserted. Figure 4 shows how the three look all assembled. Continue in this manner, passing the loop of each

unit through the loops of the two units preceding it.

5. Coil both ends of the 8 1/2-inch (21.5 cm) length until it measures 3 inches (7.5 cm) overall.

6. Bend the coils toward each other as before. Bend the loop at a right angle to the coils, and insert this longer loop (about 1 inch (2.5 cm) long) through the loops of the last two units.

7. Make a hook of the long loop like the one made for the bracelet in Chapter One, page 15.

8. Pull each coil of the assembled bracelet back into place. Using your fingers or the parallel or flat-nosed pliers, ease each coil into its original position. Start with the hook unit and work to the other end. If any are uneven, overlapping more than the others, you can even them up by coiling those that are too long and pulling the too-short ones down a bit.

9. Bend the whole bracelet so that the center ridge is higher than the edges as shown in Figure 5. This gives the bracelet a thick, rope-like look. None of the loops should show, and each unit should evenly overlap the next.

10. Make a jump ring of 16-gauge wire, and attach it to the other end from the hook. Then apply a finish of your choice.

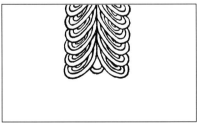

Figure 5

TO MAKE THE BRACELET LETTERED C IN FIGURE 1

This bracelet is a good one for a child or young girl.

YOU WILL NEED:

215 3/4 inches (5.4 m) of 20-gauge wire

1 inch (2.5 cm) of 18-gauge wire

1. Cut 42 lengths of 20-gauge wire, each 5 inches (12.5 cm) long. This will make a bracelet 6 1/4 inches (16 cm) long. If you wish to make a shorter or longer bracelet than this, figure the number of units based on seven units per 1 inch (2.5 cm) of bracelet. The jump ring adds about 1/4 inch (.5 cm).

2. Coil the ends of each unit toward each other until the unit measures 1 1/2 inches (4 cm) overall.

3. Make and assemble the 42 units in the same way you did those for the bracelet lettered B in Figure 1.

4. Cut one length of 20-gauge wire 5 3/4 inches (14.5 cm) long.

5. Make a hook unit the same way you made one for the bracelet in Chapter One, page 15, and attach it to the end of the bracelet.

Make and attach a jump ring of 18-gauge wire to the other end of the bracelet.

6. Apply a finish of your choice.

TO MAKE THE BRACELET LETTERED D IN FIGURE 1

YOU WILL NEED:

142 inches (3.5 m) of 16-gauge wire.

1. Cut 13 length of 16-gauge wire, each 10 inches (25.5 cm) long, and one length of 16-gauge wire 11 inches (28 cm) long.

2. Coil the ends of the 10-inch (25.5 cm) lengths toward each other until each unit measures 2 3/8 inches (6 cm) overall.

3. Make and assemble the 13 units in the same way you did the bracelet units in Chapter One, not double, the way the ones above are done.

4. Make a hook unit of the 11-inch (28 cm) length, and attach it to the end of the bracelet. Make and attach a jump ring

5. Apply a finish of your choice.

TO MAKE EARRINGS USING EGYPTIAN COILS

FOR THE EARRINGS IN FIGURE 6 YOU WILL NEED:

35 inches (89 cm) of 18-gauge wire

Two commercial earring backs.

Household cement or liquid solder

1. Cut six lengths of 18-gauge wire, each 5 inches (12.5 cm) long.

2. Coil each end of each length to fit Figure 7.

Figure 6

Figure 7

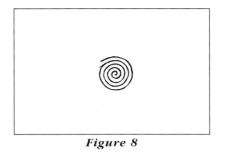

Figure 8

Figure 9

3. Use the parallel or flat-nosed pliers to flatten the center of each unit. This makes them easier to cement together.

4. Cement three units together as shown in Figure 9, using liquid solder or household cement. Be careful that they are evenly spaced. You will need a clamp like the one described in Chapter One, page 18, to hold the units in place while they are drying. Cement the other three units in the same manner.

5. Cut two lengths of 18-gauge wire, each 2 1/2 inches (6.5 cm) long for the center coils.

6. Coil these two lengths and turn the ends under, as shown in Figure 8.

7. Place one of these coils on the top of each earring, cement them from the back, and let them dry again.

8. Shape the earrings, placing one of them in the palm of your left hand and pressing gently on the center of the earring with your right thumb. This will make the earring saucer-shaped. Press

the other earring in the same manner.

9. Apply a finish of your choice.

10. Cement commercial earring back to the backs of the earrings.

FOR THE EARRINGS IN FIGURE 10 YOU WILL NEED:

9 inches (23 cm) of 14-gauge wire

20 inches (51 cm) of 18-gauge wire, or 10 inches (25.5 cm) of 18-gauge wire and two beads.

Two commercial earring backs.

1. File all the ends flat. Bend each length to fit the large curved piece in Figure 10, using the round-nosed pliers to make the top loop, your fingers to make the larger curve, and then the pliers for the other loop.

Figure 10

2. Cut two lengths of 18-gauge wire, each 4 inches (10 cm) long, and two lengths each 6 inches (15 cm) long for the coils. File one end of each length flat.

3. Coil the 4-inch (10 cm) length from the unfiled end to make the unit that hangs inside the 14-gauge unit, as shown in Figure 10, leaving 1/2 inch (1.5 cm) to be looped, as shown, at a right angle to the coil.

4. Open the loops of the 18-gauge units sideways, and assemble the units as shown in Figure 10. Apply a finish of your choice.

If, instead of the dangling coils, you wish to use beads as shown in Figure 11:

1. Cut two lengths of 18-gauge wire at least 1 inch (2.5 cm) long—longer if the beads you want to use are larger than the one shown in Figure 11.

File all the ends flat.

Loop one end of each length.

2. Insert the unlooped end of each length through the hole in the center of one of the beads. Loop the protruding end of each length.

3. After the wire units have been lacquered and are dry, open the loop on one end of each unit, and assemble the earrings as shown in Figure 11.

Figure 11

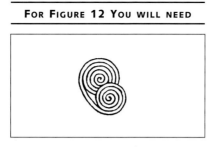

Figure 12

14 inches (36 cm) of 20 gauge wire

1. Cut two lengths of 20-gauge wire, each 7 inches (18 cm) long.

2. Coil the ends to fit Figure 12. Apply a finish.

3. Attach commercial earring backs to the larger coil of each unit, so the wire that goes around the earlobe is concealed by the smaller wire.

TO MAKE A RING USING THE EGYPTIAN COILS

YOU WILL NEED:

16 inches (40.5 cm) of 18-gauge wire

Figure 13

Figure 14

---

1. Cut a 16-inch (40.5 cm) length of 18-gauge wire.

2. Coil the ends to fit the two coils in Figure 13.

3. Wrap the wire around your finger to make four complete circles, then push the coils into place with the smaller overlapping the larger. Apply a finish.

TO MAKE A BRACELET USING EGYPTIAN COILS

YOU WILL NEED:

108 1/2 inches (2.7 m) of 18-gauge wire

1. Cut 14 lengths of 18-gauge wire, each 7 1/2 inches (19 cm) long.

2. Coil the ends of each length to fit Figure 15.

3. Using the parallel pliers, bend one-half of the units to fit Figure 16, and the other half to fit Figure 17.

4. Bend each unit so that one-half of them fit the first link on the left in Figure 14, and the other half fit the second link.

5. Cut one length of 18-gauge wire, 3 1/2 inches (9 cm) long, and make a hook as shown in Figure 14.

6. Assemble as you did the bracelet in Chapter 12, page 55, with the two kinds of links alternating, as in Figure 14. Apply a finish.

Figure 15

TO MAKE A NECKLACE USING COILS

YOU WILL NEED:

142 inches (3.5 m) of 16-gauge wire

1. Cut 20 lengths of 16-gauge wire, each 7 inches (18 cm) long.

File one end of each length round, the other flat. Loop the rounded end of each length to fit Figure 19.

2. Hold one of the lengths in the parallel pliers as shown in Figure 20. Coil the wire around itself until there are 2 1/2 rounds as shown in Figure 21. Coil the other lengths in the same way.

3. Using your fingers, bend each unit to fit Figure 21 and then to fit Figure 22, looping the end of each with the round-nosed pliers.

4. Cut one length of 16-gauge wire 2 inches (5 cm) long for the hook. Make a hook to fit Figure 23. Open the loops of each of the units and of the hook.

5. Assemble the necklace as shown in Figure 18, and attach the hook as shown in Figure 23. Apply a finish.

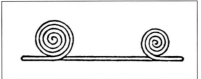

Figure 16

Figure 17

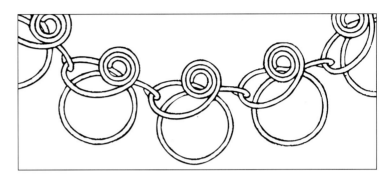

Figure 18

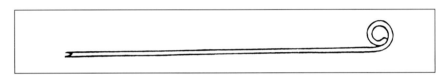

Figure 19

Figure 20

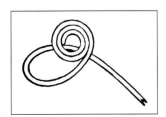

Figure 21

Figure 22

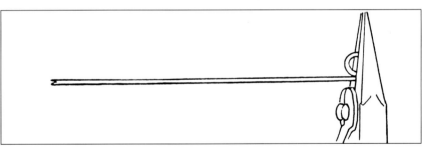

Figure 23

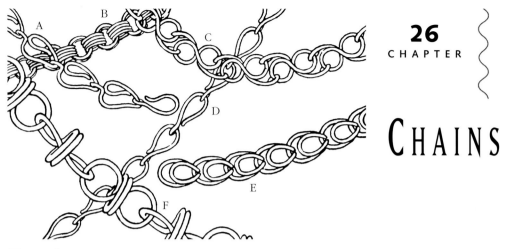

Figure 1

CHAINS

THE CONCEPT OF A CHAIN IS ELEMEN-tary—make duplicates of a design motif, link them together, and you have your finished piece. But no matter how simple this sounds, chains remain some of the most sophisticated additions to any jewelry wardrobe. Worn as is, or with dangles, lockets, or beads, chains can dress up or dress down for any occasion.

You'll notice the designs in this chapter take their shapes from previous projects. As you work, you should get a concept of how easily designs can adapt when you change the size of the links or use a different gauge of wire.

TO MAKE THE CHAIN LETTERED A IN FIGURE 1

NOTE: Two links equal approximately 1 inch (2.5 cm) of finished chain. Adjust the number of links you cut to make the finished length of chain you'll need.

YOU WILL NEED:

18-gauge wire

1. Cut as many 1 3/4-inch (4.5 cm) lengths of 18-gauge wire as you will need for the length of chain you wish to make.

2. Follow the procedure in Chapter Five, making each length into the leaf shape. Measure your work against the illustration of the chain, Figure 1 A. The hook will take 1 inch (2.5 cm) of 18-gauge wire.

TO MAKE THE CHAIN LETTERED B IN FIGURE 1

NOTE: Each link will make about 3/4 inch (2 cm) of chain

YOU WILL NEED:

20-gauge wire.

2 1/2 inches (6.5 cm) of 16-gauge wire

A mandrel 3/16 inch (4.7 mm) in diameter, the approximate size of a #8 (US) knitting needle

1. Wind 20-gauge wire around the mandrel (#8 (US) knitting needle) to make as many four-round units as you will need for the length of chain you wish to make.

2. Follow the procedure outlined in Chapter Three for making the links and assembling them. Make a hook from 1 1/2 inches (4 cm) of 16-gauge wire, and a jump ring of 16-gauge wire wound on the same mandrel you used for the chain.

TO MAKE THE CHAIN LETTERED C IN FIGURE 1

NOTE: Each link will make about 9/16 inch (1.6 cm) of chain—four will make 2 1/4 inches (5.5 cm) of chain.

YOU WILL NEED:

18-gauge wire.

A mandrel 3/16 inch (4.7 mm) in diameter, the approximate size of a #8 (US) knitting needle

1. Wind 18-gauge wire around the mandrel to make as many 3 1/2-

round units as you will need for the length of chain you wish to make.

2. Follow the procedure outlined in Chapter Seven for making the links and assembling them, measuring against Figure 1 C as you go.

3. Use a 1 1/2-inch (4 cm) length for the hook and a 1 1/4-inch (3 cm) length for the eye, making them in the same shapes as those made for the bracelet in Chapter Seven.

TO MAKE THE CHAIN LETTERED D IN FIGURE 1

NOTE: Two finished links will equal approximately 1 inch (2.5 cm).

YOU WILL NEED:

18-gauge wire

A mandrel 3/8 inch (1 cm) in diameter, the approximate size of a #15 or #16 (US) knitting needle

1. Cut as many 1 1/4-inch (3 cm) lengths of 18-gauge wire as you will need for the length of chain you wish to make.

2. Follow the procedure outlined in Chapter 22 to make each length into the shape illustrated in Figure 1 D. Use 1 1/4 inches (3 cm) of 18-gauge wire for the hook, and make a jump ring of 16-gauge wire on the mandrel (#15 or #16 (US) knitting needle).

TO MAKE THE CHAIN LETTERED E IN FIGURE 1

NOTE: Four links equal approximately 1 1/2 inch (4 cm), each individual link is approximately 3/8 inch (1 cm) long.

YOU WILL NEED:

18-gauge wire

A mandrel 3/16 inch (5 mm) in diameter, the approximate size of a #8 or #9 (US) knitting needle.

1. Cut as many 1 3/4-inch (4.5 cm) lengths of 18-gauge wire as you will need for the length of chain you wish to make.

2. Follow the procedure outlined in Chapter 23 to make and assemble the links, measuring against Figure 1 E as you go. Use 1 inch (2.5 cm) of 18-gauge wire to make a hook like the one you made for the chain marked A in Figure 1. A jump ring made of 16-gauge wire wrapped around a mandrel about 3/16 inch (4.7 mm) in diameter (#8 or #9 (US) knitting needle) should go on the other end of the chain.

TO MAKE THE CHAIN LETTERED F IN FIGURE 1

NOTE: Each link (a four-round unit) will equal approximately 3/4 inch (2 cm) of chain.

YOU WILL NEED:

14-gauge wire

A mandrel 3/8 inch (1 cm) in diameter, the approximate size of a #15 or #16 (US) knitting needle

1. Wind 14-gauge wire around the mandrel to make as many four-round units as you will need for the length of chain you wish to make.

2. Follow the procedure outlined in Chapter 14, page 68, to make and assemble the chain. Use the loop of the last unit of the chain to make a hook.

TO MAKE A CHOKER OF CHAIN IN FIGURE 2

YOU WILL NEED:

121 inches (3 m) of 14-gauge wire

A mandrel about 5/32 inch (5.7 mm) in diameter, the approximate size of a #5 (US) knitting needle

1. Cut 24 lengths of 14-gauge wire, each 5 inches (12.5 cm) long. File all the ends round.

2. Wrap each length around the mandrel, leaving about 1/2 inch (1.5 cm) of straight wire on each end, as shown in Figure 3. Be sure to wrap all the units in the same direction.

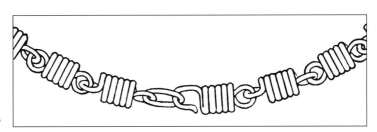

Figure 2

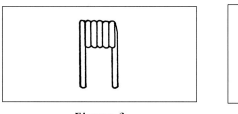

Figure 3

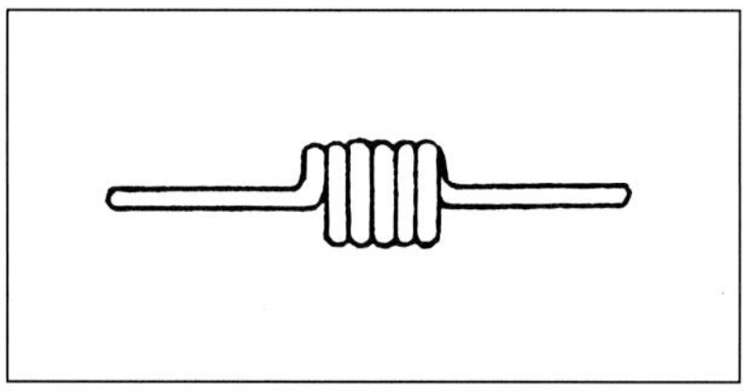

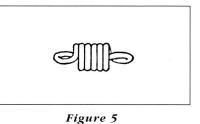

Figure 4

Figure 5

3. Using the parallel or flat-nosed pliers, bend each unit to look like Figure 4.

4. Loop the ends of each unit so that the loop lies across the open end of the spring and the tip lies close against the inside of the end round of the unit. Do not loop the second end of the last unit, but use it to make the hook. Open the loop on one end of each unit sideways.

5. Cut a jump ring from the spring you made for Chapter Three, page 22, or one like it, open the jump ring, and file its ends flat. Assemble the necklace as shown in Figure 2. Apply a finish of your choice.

NOTE: If you wish to make a longer chain of these units, you can figure the number of links needed on the basis of one link to 5/8 inch (1.6 cm) of chain.

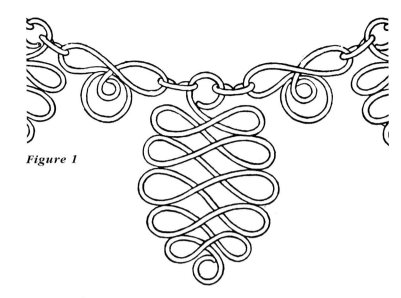

Figure 1

ADAPTATIONS

WHEN YOU CAN EASILY ADAPT THE basic principles of technique to any design, you're well on your way to creating whatever you envision. By now, you should have no trouble making designs like the necklace in this chapter with only the illustration of the finished product as measurement.

The links shown in Figure 3, on page 106, can be used for a belt or a bracelet. They show another use of a jig with a simpler method of looping the wire back and forth.

The ring in Figure 5 and the earring in Figure 6 are variations on previous designs. We hope you find them as much fun to make as the originals.

NECKLACE

YOU WILL NEED:

127 inches (3 m) of 14-gauge wire

1. Cut one 18-inch (45.5 cm) length of 14-gauge wire.

File both ends round.

2. Using the round-nosed pliers, bend the wire to fit the center unit in Figure 1. Start at the top, making sure the wire crosses itself in the same direction each time as it does in the drawing.

3. Cut two lengths of 14-gauge wire, each 13 1/2 inches (34 cm) long. File all the ends round.

4. Bend both lengths of wire to fit the left-hand unit in figure 2. One of these units will go on each side of the center unit you have just made, with small connecting links between. Remember that one will be the reverse of the other, so you must turn one over (See Figure 1).

5. Cut two lengths of 14-gauge wire, each 10 inches (25.5 cm) long.

File all the ends round.

6. Bend each 10-inch (25.5 cm) length to fit the right-hand unit in Figure 2. One of them must also be turned over when you assemble the necklace with the graduated sizes on each side of the center piece.

7. Place one of the five units you have made in the palm of your right hand. Press down on the center of it with your left thumb. This will curve the entire unit so that the edges are lower and the center higher when you turn the unit over to be assembled.

8. Curve each of these units in the same way, remembering that of each matching set of two, one must face left and one right.

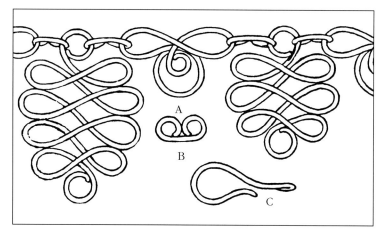

Figure 2

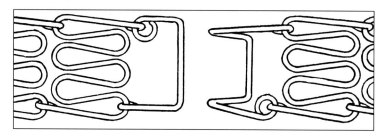

Figure 3

shows how one side of the necklace is assembled: the other side has units in the same order, but with the direction of the loops reversed. Connect the hook to one end, the jump ring to the other.

17. Apply a finish of your choice.

TO MAKE A BRACELET OR BELT OF THIS DESIGN

NOTE: Each finished link is approximately 1 inch (2.5 cm) wide. The hook and eye add approximately 1 1/2 inch (4 cm) to the over all length of the finished piece. The directions given are for the bracelet. Adjust the number of lengths you cut accordingly when making a belt.

YOU WILL NEED:

59 1/2 inches (1.5 cm) of 14-gauge wire (for the bracelet)

Jig (directions below)

1. Cut seven lengths of 14-gauge wire each 7 1/2 inches (19 cm) long. (Adjust the number you need to cut when making a belt.)

2. Make a jig from Figure 4. Follow the same procedure for making a jig as found in Chapter Nine, page 46.

3. Wrap each length of wire in turn around the jig nails, leaving

9. Cut eight lengths of 14-gauge wire, each 5 inches (12.5 cm) long.

File all the ends round.

10. Bend each length to fit the connecting link lettered A in Figure 2.

11. Cut 12 lengths of 14-gauge wire, each 1 1/2 inches (4 cm) long.

File all the ends flat.

12. Bend each of these lengths to fit the link lettered B in Figure 2. Open each loop of these units sideways. The easiest way is to open one loop in one direction, and the other in the opposite direction.

13. Cut a 2 1/2-inch (6.5 cm) length of 14-gauge wire to make the hook. File one end round, the other flat.

14. Bend the rounded end to fit the hook lettered C in Figure 2, with a loop on the flat end.

15. Cut a jump ring from the spring you made for Chapter Three, or make one by following the directions on page 22. File its ends flat, and open it.

16. Assemble the necklace, with the largest unit in the center, connected to the next A unit by a B unit, and so on, as in Figure 1 on page 105. Figure 2, on this page,

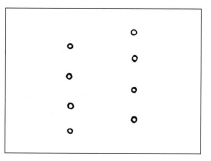

Figure 4

1/2 inch (1.5 cm) on each end to make the loops. Loop each end of each unit, as indicated in Figure 3.

5. Cut a length of 14-gauge wire 3 inches (7.5 cm) long, and one 4 inches (10 cm) long, to make the hook-and-eye clasp. Make a hook of the 4-inch (10 cm) length and an eye of the 3-inch (7.5 cm) length, and fit them against the ones in Figure 3. Assemble the bracelet or belt as shown in Figure 3.

6. Apply a finish of your choice.

DESIGN FOR RING

YOU WILL NEED:

11 inches (28 cm) of 14-gauge wire (this is an approximate measurement for an average-size finger)

One half-ball 1/2 inch (1.5 cm) in diameter, or a button of about that size.

1. Cut one length of 14-gauge wire 11 inches (28 cm) long. File the ends round.

2. Using the parallel or flat-nosed pliers, bend the length of wire about 4 inches (10 cm) from one end. Next, pinch the wire together to make the closed loop that will be on the top of the half-ball as shown in Figure 5.

3. Continue to hold the wire in the parallel or flat-nosed pliers just as they were when you finished pinching the wire together (with the 4-inch (10 cm) end away from you).

4. Bend both ends of wire around into a double circle that fits around the half-ball as shown in Figure 5, with the 4-inch (10 cm) end making the inner circle.

5. Continue to bend both ends around the outside of the first circle, until the unit looks like Figure 5.

Figure 5

6. Bend the longer end to make a right angle to the design just made, and then make three circles to go around the finger. Start from the free end and roll the wire up toward the design.

7. Bend the shorter end under, as shown in Figure 5, using the round-nosed pliers to put the end where it will help to hold the half-ball in place.

8. Apply a finish of your choice.

9. After the lacquer is dry, insert the half-ball or button by bending the top part of the design upward with your fingers and then pressing it back down into place after you insert the half-ball.

THE BIRD CAGE AGAIN

YOU WILL NEED:

25 inches (63.5 cm) of 16-gauge wire

A few balls or beads of whatever size you find convenient. (The ones shown in Figure 6 use a 5/16-inch (8 mm), a 1/4-inch (6 mm) and a 3/8-inch (9.5 mm) ball.)

Two commercial earring backs

Household cement or liquid solder

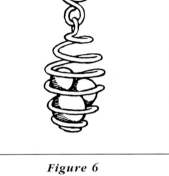

Figure 6

1. Cut two lengths of 16-gauge wire 9 inches (23 cm) long for the cages, and two lengths 3 1/2 inches (9 cm) long for the coils.

2. Coil the 3 1/2-inch (9 cm) lengths to fit the coils in Figure 6, leaving 1/2 inch (1.5 cm) to loop back as shown.

3. Make two cages of the 9-inch (23 cm) lengths. (See Chapter 19, pages 82-83, for the method.)

4. Assemble two earrings as indicated in Figure 6, without the balls. Apply a finish of your choice. When the earrings dry, open the cages to insert the balls, or beads then close them.

5. Attach commercial earring backs to the coils.

Figure 1

NEW TWISTS

READY? WE THINK YOU HAVE THE skills to try to design something on your own. Use this chapter as a guideline. The figures and text on these pages include a number of hints and ideas that will add the finishing touches to the skills you've already mastered. As you read and work through these pages, you should get an idea of how others might approach a design problem.

Take a measured length (say, 24 inches (61 cm)) of wire, make a sharp bend 3/4 inch (2 cm) from one end to hold, and doodle with the rest of it.

Don't fight the wire—let it work for you, let it help you to find attractive shapes. The patterns you create do not have to resemble anything. If you do bend it into a shape that reminds you of something, you may want to pursue a pictorial design. Many people often begin developing their ideas by drawing them.

Whatever you do, have fun. Use cheap wire (and plenty of it). If nothing appears but horrible tangles, don't let it worry you. Start over. Don't think ahead to the final

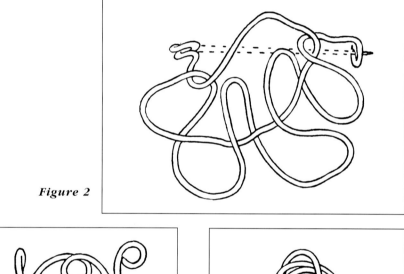

Figure 2

Figure 3

Figure 4

results yet. And learn to disregard comments from friends and family who may simply ask, "What is it?"

As you gain practice and think about designing, you'll begin to find inspiration from many sources. You may see a piece of string lying in a tangle on the floor, a chain, a

caricature drawn with a continuous line, a wrought-iron trivet, or a casual line on a scratch pad that may ignite the idea for a design.

While you're twisting the wire, remember that the best designs are always the simplest. Keep your purpose in perspective—you're designing costume pieces for casual wear. Wire jewelry, no matter how original and charming, is not suitable for formal occasions.

One of the enjoyable things about making your own designs is that there are no hard and fast rules. Some people decide before the first twist what they'll be making, whether it's a pin or bracelet. Others just twist until something happens and they see the beginnings of the first unit of a bracelet or the link in a chain.

The following hints will give you some broad guidelines that may keep you out of trouble. Use them once you decide what the piece of wire will become.

NECKLACE

Remember that the units must be shaped so that they will fit together to form a series that will lie flat and curve gracefully around the neck. Figure 3 shows a link that became the start of a necklace made of many links of graduated sizes, each different from the rest, but each made up of circles.

BRACELET

A bracelet must curve around the wrist without too much sliding from side to side. The links must be short enough to keep the bracelet flexible, and the hook should not add too much length to the whole.

RINGS

If you are designing a ring, it will be easy enough if you make sure to start with an extra-long, measured piece of wire. Wrap it around your finger a couple of times, then work out your own motif on the top.

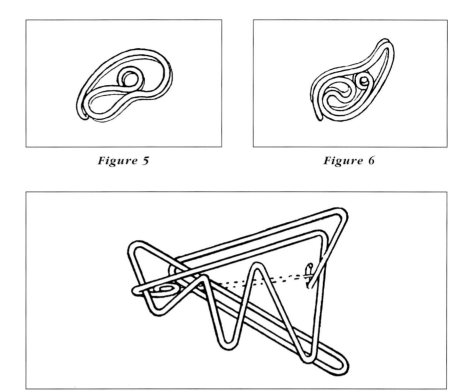

Figure 5

Figure 6

Figure 7

EARRINGS

Earrings are not a problem if you keep them lightweight. Remember, you must have a spot in the center back on which to glue the earring back or a loop on the top for attaching a wire.

Slip-on earrings are even easier. All you need to keep in mind is that the pattern should not cross the wire over itself too many times, and that you will have to repeat the same design on the other side.

LAPEL PINS

Lapel pins remain a popular accessory. Remember to start out with a 3/4-inch (2 cm) piece for the hook. Start from there and you can do almost anything—from a free, abstract design, to monograms, or a portrait of your favorite pet. Leave enough extra wire on the other end to make the pin tong. In Figure 1, the variety of width was achieved by hammering the large loops with a metal hammer on a hard surface, letting the tool marks show as a part of the design.

Do not hammer where one wire crosses over another—this will result in ugly distortions.

No matter what you make, keep track of the wire you use through careful measuring. It's always helpful to keep a notebook where you can record the amount of wire you use in each design. You can also take note of any difficult procedures. If you do this, you'll have all the information you need if you want to duplicate a piece.

GLOSSARY

ANNEALED: Softened by heat-treating.

BURR: The roughness left by a tool in cutting metal.

COIL: A flat spiral.

DRAWPLATE: A die plate through which wire is pulled to reduce its diameter.

GAUGE: A standard measure of dimensions, in this case, the diameter of wire.

JIG: A contrivance, usually of wood and nails, used as a guide for bending wire.

JUMP RING: A ring, usually round, used to join two other links.

LIVER OF SULPHUR: Potassium sulphate, used in solution to oxidize, or "antique," jewelry.

MANDREL: An axis, spindle, or core usually tapered or cylindrical, around which wire can be bent.

UNIT: A single part of a piece of jewelry which is made of several similar parts.

CONTRIBUTING ARTISTS

*THE FOLLOWING DESIGNERS PRODUCED THE
PIECES FEATURED IN THE COLOR PHOTOS
ON PAGES 33-40 AND 57-64.*

JACALYN BRULL has a B.F.A. in metal-smithing from the University of Georgia and has attended Penland School of Crafts. Her work is currently being shown in Asheville, NC, where she lives and works.

PEGGY DEBELL is a multi-talented designer working in mixed media, artwear, and photography. Her natural curiosity and far-ranging skills enable her to create art from just about anything. Her studio overlooks the skyline and mountains of Asheville, NC.

COURTNEY STEIN moved to Asheville, NC, from the North Carolina coast to set up her design studio. While she primarily enjoys silver casting, she has found wire to be an enjoyable change of pace.

ALISON THORNTON is a jewelry designer who served her apprenticeship at Old Town Silversmiths in Winchester, VA. She is currently completing her studies in the Professional Crafts Program at Haywood Community College in Clyde, NC.

TRENOR H. BENDER and **SHERRY O. HARREL** assisted Alison Thornton with project production.

ACKNOWLEDGEMENTS

Thanks to the Professional Crafts Program of Haywood Community College in Clyde, NC, with special thanks to Arch Gregory, jewelry instructor. Thanks also to Dana Irwin for lending her design expertise during photography, Carol Taylor for editorial support and Kathy Holmes for production assistance..

INDEX

RELATED TITLES FROM LARK BOOKS

Great Wire Jewelry
Projects & Techniques

By Irene From Petersen

$14.95 Hardcover ($21.95 Can.) 80 color illustrations, 10 photos

ISBN 1-57990-093-3

Distributed by Random House

Make Your Own Great Earrings
Beads, Wire, Polymer Clay, Fabric, Found Objects

By Jane LaFerla

128 Pages, 57 color photos, 55 b&w photos

$14.95 Paperback ($21.95 Can.) ISBN 1-57990-041-3

Distributed by Random House

Textile Techniques in Metal
For Jewelers, Textile Artists, & Sculptors

By Arline M. Fisch

160 pages, 60 color plates

$26.95 Hardcover ($39.95 Can.) ISBN 0-937274-93-3

Distributed by Random House